or beginners; and I have no doubt that the principal Agents of the Comany would gladly incur the expense of a large number of copies for suplying their Canvassers with it, were it brought to their notice."

The following is from the BANKING AND INSURANCE CHRONICLE, Chicago:

"On every page of this work is information of which no Life Insurance agent or solicitor should be ignorant if he expects to succeed in his calling. Indeed, we have never seen set forth with such clearness the reasons why some men do not succeed in the getting of Life Insurance policies. Dr. Fish takes that high standard for the moral dignities of the profession of Life Assurance to which it is fully entitled, and in all of the sixty-four rules for 'Beginning,' 'Managing,' and 'Enlarging' the business, as well as 'Arguments in urging Assurance,' and 'How to meet Objections,' he gives methods for the guidance of the agent and the solicitor, which are ennobling alike to the profession and the practitioner."

An effective General Agent writes: "I have perused every section of the Agent's Manual with much interest. It not only meets my views of what a Life Insurance Agent should be, and do, but it certainly is a work very much needed among the 'Profession.' In my judgment Companies would do good service to their cause by putting a copy into the hands of *every agent they commission.*"

Another writes: "*It is indeed invaluable.*"

Another writes: "So full, apt, and forcible are the numerous hints, arguments, and suggestions, with the different items of information, contained in the Agent's Manual of Life Assurance, that if one will but read and put in practice what is here furnished, he *cannot fail of success.*"

Another experienced General Agent writes: "Every word is true and fitting. *Had I read this book four years ago, it would now have been worth to me a thousand dollars.*" [OVER.

RATES BY THE FIFTY COPIES.

Grade No.	1,	square 8vo,	muslin, antique, blue and gold, tinted paper, each			....	$2 00
do	2,	do	paper covers, red edges,	do	do	....	1 75
do	3,	small 8vo,	muslin, antique, do	do	do	....	1 50
do	4,	do	paper covers, do	do	do	....	1 25
do	5,	square 12mo,	do common style throughout			....	1 10

OTHER RATES.

Ten per cent. will be added to the above rates where less than 50 copies are ordered at a time; and ten per cent. will be deducted where over 300 copies are ordered at a time. Single copies will be sent by mail, postage prepaid, upon receipt of the price and ten cents extra for postage.

☞ In ordering, be particular to specify *which grade* is wanted.

The author (Rev. Dr. Fish) can be addressed, *care of the publishers*, as above; but all orders and business communications, to secure immediate attention, must be addressed to the *publishers*, as below.

If desired, the Company's *imprint*, and also that of the General Agent, if so requested, will be added, without expense, where fifty or more copies are ordered at a time.

Any Clerk, Secretary, Agent, or Officer of a Company who will engage to see that a circular descriptive of the Agent's Manual is put into the hands of every Agent and Canvasser of the Company, by so informing the publishers, as above, will receive by mail, *with copies of the circulars*, a handsome muslin bound copy of the AGENT'S MANUAL in blue and gold, without charge. *State the number of circulars wanted.*

THE AMERICAN MANUAL OF LIFE ASSURANCE,

(By the author of the Agent's Manual of Life Assurance,) a little book of 54 pages 12mo has been wonderfully successful as a *canvassing* document. An Agent says: "*It hits every time.*"

Price, in Illuminated covers and tinted paper, single copies, and less than 100, 20 cents each; 100 copies and less than 1000, each 18 cents; 1000 copies and less than 5000, 15 cents each; 5000 copies or over, 13 cents each. No charge for inserting Company's matter, except type-setting. Address as *below*, being careful to designate *American* Manual (to distinguish it from *Agent's* Manual).

☞ The author has prepared a small condensed *German* edition of this Manual, which can be furnished in beautiful style, with the Company's matter, at from $60 to $80 per 1000 copies. Sample copies for examination will be sent upon application. Orders for any of the above works must be sent to

WYNKOOP & HALLENBECK,
Printers and Publishers,
113 Fulton street, N. Y.

EXCLUSIVELY FOR AGENTS.

THE

AGENT'S MANUAL

OF

BY THE AUTHOR OF "THE AMERICAN MANUAL OF LIFE ASSURANCE," AND PRIZE ESSAYS "PRIMITIVE PIETY REVIVED," "THE GREAT INQUIRY ANSWERED," "DON'T SWEAR," AND "THE HOUR FOR ACTION."

MUTUAL LIFE INSURANCE CO. OF NEW YORK,
NO. 144 BROADWAY.

EXCLUSIVELY FOR AGENTS.

THE

AGENT'S MANUAL

OF

BY THE AUTHOR OF "THE AMERICAN MANUAL OF LIFE ASSURANCE," AND PRIZE ESSAYS "PRIMITIVE PIETY REVIVED," "THE GREAT INQUIRY ANSWERED," "DON'T SWEAR," AND "THE HOUR FOR ACTION."

MUTUAL LIFE INSURANCE CO. OF NEW YORK,

NO. 144 BROADWAY.

"Among the honorable workers in the civilized world, to whom the public as well as the assured will die indebted, we give faithful and successful Life Assurance Agents a high place."

ELIZUR WRIGHT.

"That some of the tears of the widow may be wiped away, and some of the cries of the fatherless be hushed."

PREFATORY NOTE.

EVERY science has its corresponding art. Life Assurance is a Science; but it is also an Art. The theory is one thing; the practice is quite another. And the latter is not a matter of less importance than the former.

As a consequence, active and intelligent AGENTS are essential to the prosperity of a Life Company. It is not enough to establish agencies. Those filling them are to be instructed and stimulated into full-grown and efficient men.

Every successful and rising Assurance office has devoted a considerable part of its attention to the matter of agencies. Where this has been deemed of trifling moment, little has been accomplished.

A Life Agency may fairly be called a *Profession*. And hence an agent should have, besides a general education, a sort of *professional* education,—which, by common consent is demanded in the practice of law, medicine and the like. Other things being equal, the more familiar one is with his profession, the more thoroughly furnished is he for his work.

The public is fast becoming enlightened on the subject of Life Assurance. Inquisitive minds now push their investigations beyond the advertisements, circulars, &c., of the Life Companies, and ask for other information. Hence, a higher grade of intelligence and capacity on the part of agents is requisite;—just as the general education of the masses necessitates a more thorough education of the teachers. They must broaden the horizon of their knowledge, and be prepared to speak intelligently of what they recommend. In a word, they must show that they are *masters* of their profession. For how can a novice instruct? And how can an agent bring to bear a controlling influence upon a man who is competent to be his teacher in the very things belonging to his occupation?

A work like that here submitted was therefore needed. Its aim is one and simple;—namely, *to help Life Assurance Agents.* It puts into their hands just the facts they want to possess; gives them something to think about; furnishes a multitude of hints and suggestions; magnifies their work and places it on a higher level; raises their courage; kindles enthusiasm; and imparts force, readiness, and effectiveness in their high and beneficent calling.

The author takes occasion to acknowledge his indebtedness to the Hon. Wm. Barnes, Insurance Commissioner for the State of New York, Mr. J. G. Batterson, President of the Travelers' Insurance Company, Hartford, Conn., Mr. Lewis C. Lawton, Assistant Actuary of the Mutual Life Insurance of New York, and other gentlemen, whose statistical and other publications, and whose kind assistance, have given increased value to this work.

CONTENTS.

I.

PAGE.

THE SIGNIFICATION OF TERMS 11

II.

THE LITERATURE OF LIFE ASSURANCE 15

III.

THE HISTORY OF LIFE ASSURANCE 19

IV.

THE NAMES, OFFICERS, ETC., OF EXISTING CO'S .. 25

V.

THE SCIENCE OF LIFE ASSURANCE 31

VI.

THE PRACTICE ELUCIDATED 37

VII.

PAGE.
THE MORAL ASPECT OF LIFE OPERATIONS 43

VIII.

THE QUALITIES OF A GOOD AGENT 47

1. He appreciates his work 47
2. He is moved by high impulses 49
3. His heart is enlisted 51
4. He is active and industrious 52
5. He is courageous and determined 54
6. He has tact and discrimination 56
7. He speaks the truth 58
8. He has a good reputation 61
9. He is agreeable in manners 62
10. He is devoted to his calling 64
11. His interest is in one Company 65
12. He is careful in selecting risks 64

IX.

BEGINNING THE BUSINESS 67

1. Personal canvass at the outset 67
2. A policy on his own life 68
3. Familiarity with Life Assurance 69
4. Posted as to his own Company 70
5. His Medical Examiner 70

PAGE.

6. Acquaintances registered and visited. 71
7. Making new acquaintances 72
8. Getting names for reference 73
9. Treatment of other Agents 74

X.

MANAGING THE BUSINESS 75
1. Method in everything 75
2. Relations to the Home Office 76
3. Satisfied with terms 77
4. Prompt delivery of Policies 78
5. Renewals and rejections 78
6. Helping the Hesitating 79
7. Filling out applications 79
8. Resign if doing nothing 80

XI.

ENLARGING THE BUSINESS 81
1. Widening one's own field 81
2. Striking for large Policies 82
3. Depending on "Machinery." 83
4. Editorial notices. 84
5. The use of Reports, Office-books, &c. 84
6. The influence of Ministers 85

PAGE.

7. Sunday-School Teachers 86
8. Turning to advantage deaths of assured 86
9. Same of the deaths of unassured 87
10. New attention to canvassing 87
11. The motive of patronage 88
12. Never without blank applications 88
13. Recommending new Agents, ... 89
14. Operating through "bosses" and employees 89
15. Visiting the "intimate friend," 90
16. Convincing the Wives 90
17. Looking after the newly married 91
18. Making each assured a helper 92
19. Applying to those already assured 92

XII.

ARGUMENTS IN URGING ASSURANCE 93

1. Scripture and duty 94
2. Immediate provision 95
3. It is found here 95
4. The only method known 95
5. Uncertainty of life 96
6. Posibility of sickness 96
7. Family affection 97
8. A social obligation 97

PAGE.
9. Its beneficence 98
10. A means of self-protection 98
11. Variety of uses 99
12. A good investment 100
13. Increases credit 101
14. Personal Advantages 101
15. Joy to the Household 102
16. A dictate of prudence 102
17. Final appeal 103

XIII.

HOW TO MEET OBJECTIONS 115
1. Indebtedness 105
2. Well off 106
3. Religious scruples 106
4. Fears as to safety 107
5. Expensiveness 108
6. Making money 108
7. Assuring one's self 109
8. The Savings Bank 109
9. Using funds in business 110
10. No family ties 111
11. Inability to continue 111
12. Some other time 111

XIV.

PAGE.
CONVENIENT TABLES............ 113
1. Interest and Discount.......... 113
2. Compound Interest No. 1 114
3. Compound Interest No. 2.......... 116
4. Description of Standard Mortality Tables 120
5. Breslau Table.......... 124
6. London Table.......... 125
7. Swedish Table.......... 126
8. French Table 127
9. Northampton Table 128
10. Carlisle Table.......... 129
11. Equitable Table.......... 130
12. Belgian Table.......... 131
13. Combined Experience Table 132
14. English Table No. 1 133
15. English Table No. 2 134
16. English Table No. 3 135
17. Height and Weight.......... 136
18. Short Rule of Expectation 137
19. Discount Table.......... 138
20. Comparative Mortality Table, I.......... 139
21. Comparative Mortality Table, II.......... 140
22. Comparative Mortality Table, III.......... 141

XV.

ORIGIN AND BUSINESS OF COMPANIES.........142

Agent's Manual.

THE SIGNIFICATION OF TERMS.

ACTUARY.—In *law*, this word was originally used to designate a clerk, or registrar, in courts of civil jurisdiction. Webster defines an actuary as "the manager of a joint-stock company, particularly of an insurance company;—in America, chiefly applied to the manager of a life insurance company." A better definition is, one engaged in what are termed contingent, or accidental calculations and estimates.

Annuity—Is an annual payment; or, a yearly income charged on the person or company granting it.

Assets—Constitute the entire property of all kinds belonging to a person or an association.

Assurance, or *Insurance*—Is a contract for the payment of a sum of money on occasion of a certain event, as loss, or death. In England, and, to an increasing extent, in America, *assurance* is used in life operations, and *insurance* in those of fire. The distinction, as made by Mr. Babbage, is this: Assurance is a contract dependent on the duration of life, which must either wholly happen or wholly fail. Insurance is a contract relating to any other uncertain event, which may *partly* happen or *partly* fail. Quite generally, however, the words interchange. Life Assurance may be defined to be a *plan by which any sum of money may be secured at death, whenever that may take place, or be received at any given age of the life assured if the life continue.*

Bonus—Is an extra dividend to the shareholders of a company, out of accumulated profits.

Dividend—Is the share of profits, or surplus, belonging to each partner or proprietor.

Loading—Is a sum added to a previous amount to make its sufficiency doubly sure

Policy—Is a ticket, warrant, or written contract for money in a public fund or society.

Premium—Is the sum paid for insurance or indemnity. By

Single Premium is meant a sum of money paid down, and in consideration of which, without any further payment, the sum assured will be guaranteed to be paid at any given age, or at the death of the assurer. By Annual Premium is meant a sum of money to be paid yearly until the death of the party, or for a limited number of years, as may be agreed upon.

Reserve.—This is the difference between the present value of the sum assured and the present value of the net future premiums. It is that sum for which the Policy to which it belongs could be transferred to and reassured by another company.

Reversion—Is the sum payable at death, or at any future period. It may be secured by the payment of a single or of an annual premium.

Reversionary Addition.—That sum which is added to a Policy for the Cash Dividend at the single payment rate. The amount so added is payable with the original policy.

Scrip—Is a certificate of stock, or of a share of joint property.

Void—Means empty, null, having no binding force. All Life Assurance Companies have certain conditions, restrictions, or rules, the violation of which hazards or destroys the policy. These restrictions relate to travel or residence in other countries; the payment of premiums when due, &c. If these regulations are disregarded, or if the party assured dies by the hands of justice, or in an attempt to violate the law of any country where he may reside or happen to be, or in consequence of a duel, or by reason of intemperance from the use of intoxicating liquors, or by his own hand; or if the annual premium be not paid in the manner prescribed, the policy is in most of these cases, either in whole or in part, forfeited.

LITERATURE OF LIFE ASSURANCE.

FOR the most part those who have written upon the subject of Life Assurance, have done so with the purpose either of developing its laws and foundation principles, or of exhibiting its calculations. Hence their writings are chiefly abstract and scientific. English authorship is the principal field of the Literature of Life Asssurance. America has yet to produce its first decidedly great work on this subject. The publications enumerated, present a pretty complete catalogue of all works of any importance on the Assurance of human life that have ever been written.

Griffith Davies on Annuities.

F. Bailey on Annuities.

Richard Price on Annuities (2 vols.)

Quetelet on the Theory of Probabilities.

An Essay on Probabilities, by A. De Morgan.

Sang's Essay on Life Assurance.

Sang's Valuation of Life Contingencies.

Jones on Annuities and Reversionary Payments (2 vols.)

The Sixth and Twelfth Reports of the Registrar-General of England.

Pocock's Chronological List of Books on the Doctrine of Chances.

The Insurance Guide and Hand-book, 2d ed.; useful.

Charles Babbage's Tables of Logarithms.

Joshua Milne on Annuities.

E. Baylis on the Arithmetic of Annuities.

Robertson on Life Assurance.

William Morgan on Life Assurance.

Alfred Burt on Life Assurance.

Edward Hully on Life Assurance.

Hoyle on Life Assurance.

Park on Life Assurance.

Neison on Vital Statistics.

Ansell on Vital Statistics.

Ellison on Life Insurance.

Dowdeswell on Life Insurance.

Millar on Life Insurance.

E. J. Farren on Life Insurance.

A. Scratchley on Life Assurance Societies.

Thackeray on Life Assurance.

James (J. H.) on Life Assurance.

The Handbook of Life Assurance, by C. B. Norton.

The Vade Mecum, by J. Baxter Langley, M. R. S. C.

The American Manual of Life Assurance, by Henry C. Fish, D. D., Newark, N. J.

The American Life Assurance Magazine (Quarterly), by G. E. Currie, 153 Broadway (seven bound volumes).

The Insurance Monitor, by T. Jones, Jr., 14 & 16 Wall st., N. Y. (monthly, and back numbers).

The Wall Street Underwriter, by Grierson & Ecclesine, 18 Wall st. (Life and Fire), monthly.

Insurance Reports (New York and Mass.), bound volumes.

Journal of the Actuaries; monthly, London.

Francis Corbeaux on Laws of Vitality, &c.

Law of Fire and Life Insurance, Geo. D. B. Beaumont.

Assurance Premiums, by Wm. Orchard.

Life Assurance Manual, by P. A. Eagle.

Farr's New Life Tables. Quarto, 1864.

An Appeal for Life Insurance, by G. E. Currie, N. Y.

Annals, Anecdotes, etc., of Life Assurance, by J. Francis.

The Law of Life Assurance, by Charles John Bunyan.

Fifteen Years' Experience in a Mutual Life Insurance Company, by S. Homans, New York.

What is Life Assurance? by Jenkin Jones.

The Medical Selection of Lives, by Wm. Brinton.

Medical Estimate of Life, by S. H. Ward.

Hutton's Mathematical Tables.

George Cardwell: a Life Insurance Tale, by N. D. Morgan.

Marshall's Tables of Value of Annuities.

Hodgson's Observations on Duration of Life.

Why Should I Insure my Life? by H. R. Sharman.

Practical Life Tables, by Alex. McKean.

Price's Observations on Reversionary Payments.

Commission Profits of Life Assurance, by S. Brown.

Treatise on Life Annuities, by F. Blayney.

New and General Notation of Life Contingencies, by Hardy.

Peter Gray's Tables of Life Contingencies.

W. E. Hillman's Tables of Life Policies.

David Jones on Value of Annuities.

B. H. Todd's Life Insurance Investigation Tables.

W. T. Thompson's Actuarial Tables.

William Wood's Conversion Tables.

Popular Tables, by Charles M. Willich.

Medical Examinations for Life Insurance, by J. Adams Allen, Chicago, Ill.

Banking and Insurance Chronicle, Chicago, Ill.

Chisholm's Commutation Tables (2 vols.)

THE HISTORY AND PRESENT POSITION OF LIFE ASSURANCE.

DOUBT hangs over the actual origin of the idea and the practice of *insurance.* In the year 1435 a Spanish writer issued a challenge to the world, claiming for Barcelona the honor of being the birthplace of this practice. The claim was met by the Italians, who quoted the rates of insurance on shipments from London to Pisa and Bruges as early as 1400. It was also ascertained by a chronicle of King Ferdinand that the contract of reciprocal insurance was known in Portugal as early as 1375. Many other writers allude to the practice of indemnifying ship-owners and merchants against losses by the elements, or by enemies, at a much earlier date.

The invention of the *principle* of insurance has generally been accorded to the Romans, from the fact that the writings of Livy, Suetonius, Cicero, and Sallust mention stipulations of indemnity to contractors during the second Punic War, and a like surety granted by Claudius for delivery of grain during a time of great scarcity, as also the security claimed by Cicero for the carriage and safe delivery of the spoils of war gained by the victories in Silesia. The first English statute appears in the time of Ellzabeth, 1601, but it designates the system as of "tyme out of mynde, and a usage amongste merchants." The question of priority must therefore be accorded to *marine insurance*, and the invention to the Italians.

LIFE Assurance, also, dates far back in the annals of the past. It is common for writers on this subject to assign its origin to the beginning of the eighteenth century; making its existence hitherto to have been about one hundred and fifty years. But it has certainly existed twice that length of time. Indeed, we find traces of the theory of *probabilities*, (which underlies life assurance,) as far back as the time of Pliny, and even Plato, preceding the Christian era. It is also certain that some four hundred years after Christ, a table was actually in existence by which annuities could be valued.

But that Life Assurance was absolutely practiced as early

as above stated, *i. e.* in the sixteenth century, is put beyond question by the contents of a volume in the French language called the GUIDON (guide, standard), whose author is unknown, but which must have been written some three hundred years since. In this ancient document the writer speaks of "*insurance* made by some nations upon *the life of men*, in case of their decease upon a voyage, to pay certain sums to their heirs or creditors." Hence it appears that in his day "some nations" practiced life assurance. How much earlier we do not know.

From an old English work on *Usury*, printed in 1584, we learn that a particular feature of life assurance—endowments for children—supposed to be a very modern idea, was known and substantially practiced then (nearly three hundred years ago). The writer speaks of money being invested in a "Companie," which company agrees "that whosoever lendeth such a summe of money, and hath a childe of one yeere, shall have for his childe, if the same childe doo live till he be full fifteene years of age, 500 li. (pounds) of money."

We also find historical traces of the practice of assuring lives in Germany, of an equally early date.

The first scheme of importance, however, and which may be regarded as the foundation of the modern system of life contingencies, was the system of Tontines, invented by Lorenzo Tontie, or Tontine, a Neapolitan, in 1653.

The first public office for assuring lives which we are able to identify, originated with a clergyman of Middletown, Lancashire, England, named William Assheton, D. D., in the year 1698. His object was the benefit of the widows of clergymen and others, and for settling jointures and annuities. It went into operation under the name of "The Mercer's Company," in London. In 1700 another society was instituted called the "Society of Insurance of Widows and Orphans."

In the year 1706, the "Amicable Society of London" was founded; but it made this fundamental error, that the rates of premium were uniform for all ages assured; nor was any fixed amount guaranteed in case of death. Hence very little was done. In 1721 the "Royal Exehange," and "London Assurance" Companies were formed. But it was not until 1780 that the business of Life Assurance may be said to have fairly begun. In that year the "Equitable Society" (which eighteen years before had obtained a charter with the greatest difficulty, and had so far met with little success, so great was the ignorance prevailing upon the whole subject) adopted the Northampton tables as the basis of its calculations; its actuary or manager being William Morgan, who was aided by the advice of his uncle, Dr.

Richard Price, a celebrated writer upon the principles of Life Assurance.

Life Assurance was introduced into this country before the war of the Revolution. It was effected by a few Episcopalian clergymen who formed a society in 1769, called "The Protestant Episcopal Association for the Benefit of Widows and Children of Clergymen of the Commonwealth of Pennsylvania." The first *public* Assurance Company was the Pennsylvania, established in 1812, still flourishing. The Massachusetts Hospital Life Insurance Company seems to have been the next formed, in the year 1818. The New York Life Insurance and Trust Company was chartered in 1830, and the New England Mutual Life Insurance Company of Boston in 1844. But little attention, however, was paid to the subject in this country prior to 1843, at which time the Mutual Life of New York and several other companies went into successful operation.

At the present time there are in Great Britain nearly two hundred such companies; and the amount there assured upon life is estimated at £225,000,000.

In the United States there are about seventy Life Companies, receiving an annual income of nearly $50,000,000. But little short of four hundred thousand lives are now assured, covering risks amounting to about $1,000,000,000. These are striking proofs of the popularity of Life Assurance. During each year, more than *six millions* of dollars are paid by the Life Companies in the United States to the families or representatives of the assured; mainly to widows and orphans.

The number of policies now issued, yearly, by all the Companies in the United States, is not far from 120,000. And the business is constantly and rapidly increasing.

A few words may be added on the *stability* of Life Assurance. It is too much to say that Life Companies have never failed. In England, up to the time of Richard Price (1780), assurance of life had been little better than a gambling operation. And much later, has there been great unfairness in business of this description; which, happily, is not true at present. A very few Companies doing life business in this country, have by mismanagement gone down; but the cause has been the union of *other business* with that of life. Not a single Company confining itself to its legitimate work has failed, nor is the thing conceivable, for there is scarcely room for contingencies. The experience of the commercial world can point to no such permanency as is seen in Life Companies, nor does any class of institutions compare with them for uniformity, safety, and reliability.

LIFE ASSURANCE COMPANIES.

WE have spared no pains to be able to present here a full and complete list of the several Life offices in the United States. Such a list, it is believed, is found in no other publication. For reference, and correspondence, it will be of great convenience, besides the satisfaction that one feels in being "*posted.*" We arrange them in alphabetical order.

Of the officers, it will be understood that the one first named is *President*, and the next, *Secretary.*

Ætna . . . . .Hartford, Conn.
E. A. Bulkeley, T. O. Enders.

American Mutual . . . . .New Haven, Conn.
Benj. Silliman, Benj. Noyes.

American Life and Trust . . .Philadelphia.
A. Whilidin, J. S. Wilson.

American Popular . . . . .New York city.
V. M. Rice, J. Pierpont, Jr.

Atlantic Mutual . . . . .Albany, N. Y.
R. H. Pruyn, L. B. Smith.

Baltimore . . . . .Baltimore, Md.
J. I. Donaldson.

Berkshire . . . . .Pittsfield, Mass.
T. F. Plunket, B. Chickering.

British General . . . . New York city.
Branch office.

Brooklyn . . . . .Brooklyn, N. Y.
C. W. Bouck, R. H. Harding.

Cincinnati Mutual . . . . .Cincinnati, Ohio.
C. G. Megrue, G. F. Reynolds.

Charter Oak . . . . .Hartford, Conn.
J. C. Walkley, S. H. White.

Connecticut General . . . . . .Hartford, Conn.
E. W. Parsons, T. W. Russell.

Connecticut Mutual . . . . . .Hartford, Conn.
Guy R. Phelps, W. S. Olmsted.

Continental of N. Y. . . . . . .New York city.
Justus Lawrence, J. P. Rogers.

Continental of Hartford . .Hartford, Conn.
J. S. Rice, S. E. Elmore.

COVENANT MUTUAL.........St. Louis, Mo.
G. B. Allen.

ECONOMICAL MUTUAL ....Providence, R. I.
S. S. Bucklin, W. Y. Potter.

EMPIRE MUTUAL..............Chicago. Ill.

EQUITABLE ....New York city.
William C. Alexander, James W. Alexander.

EXCELSIOR...............New York city.
Samuel T. Howard, Sidney Ward.

GERMANIA ....New York city.
H. Wesendonck, F. Schwendler.

GIRARD ANNUITY & TRUST...Philadelphia.
T. Ridgway.

GLOBE MUTUAL............New York city.
Pliny Freeman, H. C. Freeman.

GREAT SOUTHERN & WESTERN.New Orleans, La.
Gen. Longstreet.

GREAT WESTERN...........New York city.
R. Bage, E. Dwight Kendall.

GUARDIAN ....New York city.
W. H. Peckham, H. V. Gahagan.

HAHNEMANN...............Cleveland, Ohio.
H. M. Chapin, A. S. Mills.

HOME....................Brooklyn.
W. S. Griffith, G. C. Ripley.

HOSPITAL................Boston, Mass.
Moses Hale, Sec.

JOHN HANCOCK............Boston, Mass.
G. P. Sanger, G. B. Ager.

KENTUCKY MUTUAL ....Cincinnati, Ohio.
J. C. Beck, A. C. Dunlap.

KNICKERBOCKER ....New York city.
E. Lyman, G. F. Sniffen.

LIFE & ACCIDENT...........Hartford, Conn.
T. J. Vail, William S. Manning,

LIVERP'L & LOND. GLOBE F. & L. New York city, branch.
A. C. Pell, Agent.

MANHATTAN ....New York city.
Henry Stokes, J. L. Halsey.

MASSACHUSETTS MUTUAL.....Springfield, Mass.
Caleb Price, F. B. Bacon.

MINERS' LIFE & TRUST Co ...Pottsville, Pa.
Jacob Huntzinger, Alfred Huntzinger.

MUTUAL OF N. Y...........New York city.
F. S. Winston, Isaac Abbatt, John M. Stuart.

MUTUAL OF CHICAGO........Chicago, Ill.
Merril Ladd, C. B. Holmes.

MUTUAL BENEFIT...........Newark, N. J.
L. C. Grover, E. A. Strong.

NATIONAL OF VERMONT......Montpelier, Vt.
J. Y. Dewey.

NATIONAL.................New York city.
E. A. Jones, John A. Mortimore.

NATIONAL LIFE & HEALTH....Kalamazoo, Mich.
S. P. Sheldon, G. W. Snyder.

NATIONAL TRAVELERS'.......New York city.
James R. Dow, J. H. Taylor.

NEW ENGLAND MUTUAL......Boston, Mass.
B. F. Stevens, J. M. Gibbons.

New Jersey Mutual........Newark, N. J.
J. P. Bradley, William M. Simpson.

New York................New York city.
Morris Franklin, W. H. Beers.

New York State Mutual...Syracuse, N. Y.
John Peck, G. P. Gardner.

New York Life & Trust....New York city.
David Thompson, P. R. Kearney.

North America ....New York city.
N. D. Morgan, J. W. Merrill.

North-Western Mutual....Milwaukee, Wis.
S. S. Dagget, A. W. Kellog.

Ohio ....Cincinnati, Ohio.
Augustus Isham.

Penn Mutual.............Philadelphia.
James Traquair, H. S. Stephens.

Pennsylvania ....Philadelphia.
Charles Dutilh, Pres't.

Philadelphia Fire & Life....Philadelphia, Pa.
R. P. King, F. Blackburn.

Phœnix Mutual...........Hartford, Conn.
E. Fessenden, J. F. Burns.

Provident Life & Trust....Philadelphia, Pa.
S. R. Shipley, Pres't.

Provident Life & Investment Chicago, Ill.
Ira Y. Munn, C. Holland.

Royal F. & L. ....New York city, branch.
A. B. McDonald, Agent.

SECURITY LIFE & ANNUITY . . . New York city.
R. L. Case, I. H. Allen.

SOUTHERN . . . . Memphis, Tenn.
G. W. McCarn, J. B. Dodds.

STATE MUTUAL . . . . Worcester, Mass.
Isaac Davis, C. Harris.

ST. LOUIS MUTUAL . . . . St. Louis, Mo.
D. A. January, W. T. Selby

TRAVELLERS' (LIFE AND ACCIDENT) . . . Hartford, Conn.
J. G. Batterson, R. Dennis.

UNIVERSAL . . . . New York city.
William Walker, J. H. Bewley.

UNION MUTUAL OF MAINE . . . . Augusta, Me.
H. Crocker, W. H. Hollister

UNITED STATES . . . . New York city.
J. B. Collins, Jno. Eadie.

WASHINGTON . . . . New York city.
Cyrus Curtiss, W. A. Brewer, Jr.

WESTERN . . . . Cincinnati, Ohio.

WIDOWS' & ORPHANS' BENEFIT. . New York city.
Charles H. Raymond, H. B. Robinson.

WORLD MUTUAL. . . . . New York city.
George L. Willard, C. W. Plyer.

☞ **It is proper to state that a few of the above Companies are doing no *new* business, but merely taking care of obligations already assumed.**

THE SCIENCE OF LIFE ASSURANCE.

SOME grand foundation principle lies at the base of every science. This we know to be true of theology, medicine, jurisprudence, political economy and the like.

Now, what is the fundamental principle of Life Assurance, as a Science? It is this:—the LAW OF AVERAGE.

We will make this plain.

By the word *law* (as *law* of nature, *law* of gravitation, and the like) is meant, the *regular method* by which certain effects follow certain conditions, or causes. When we have ascertained *how*, or in what manner, or in what relative proportion, certain effects follow certain causes, then we say we have found out the *law* regulating such and such things: as when observing men determined the *laws* regulating electricity, the tides, steam, trade, falling bodies, and the like.

Now, is there a *law* regulating the rate of mortality, or the falling of human lives in the aggregate? We should suppose so, beforehand, since nothing seems left to chance. Every thing appears to be *governed, controlled, regulated:* only sometimes the law, or rule, respecting the occurrence is too hidden to be detected. It is generally agreed that what we call chance is merely *direction not understood.*

> "All nature is but art unknown to thee,
> All chance direction which thou canst not see."

Just how many and what kinds of accidents (as they are called) and *crimes,* even, will occur among a given population during a year, for instance, can be determined with certainty beforehand. Just how many letters will be mailed undirected (from haste or carelessness in correspondents) out of any large number of letters, can be known beforehand, on the ground that what has occurred will recur. Again, it is demonstrated that just such a relative number of white and black balls, in a given number of drawings, will be taken from an urn where they are mixed promiscuously. This has been found out by actual experiment.

Or, throw into the air some thousand times a number of pennies, say fifteen hundred. It can be reckoned beforehand just how many "heads" and how many "tails," in the whole number of throwings, will be up or down. Nothing would be more uncertain than whether it wou'd be "head" or "tail" in *one* throwing of *one* penny; but the *average* in many throwings of many pennies can be got at exactly.

We should *expect*, then, that there would be a law regulating the falling of human lives, so that we could *average* them, or *get the proportion* of them;—so many out of such a number falling in a given time.

And *this we find to be the case.* The duration of any *one* life cannot, of course, be known; but that of a *multitude* of lives is easily ascertained. Or, to change the expression, nothing is more *uncertain* than the duration of *individual* life: nothing is more *certain* than the *average* continuance of life. In the same age and same country the rate of mortality from pestilence, war, &c., &c., may vary; but even these variations are doubtless governed by fixed laws; and looking at all periods and all countries, the variation does not exist.

The facts proving these statements have been brought to light by the study of statistics. For upwards of 200 years, tables have been kept in different parts of the world, to a greater or less extent, showing the births and deaths of individuals. These are generally called tables of mortality; and upon these the duration of life has been calculated with almost unerring accuracy.

By these it is ascertained, for instance, that if we take 10,000 persons in the prime of life, 1,200 will die the first ten years; 1,500 the next ten; 1,700 the next ten; and so on till all have passed away. 10,000 persons at the age of 25 years will attain the age of 62 years on an average; at the age of 35, 65 years; at the age of 45, 68; at the age of 55, 71. The average age at death of all born, is about 33 years. Or we may say that any 1,000 persons in ordinary health at the age of 25 will yet live to *average* about 37½ years each; at the age of 30, about 34½; and at the age of 35, just 31 years each; and so on.

Now, calculations having reference to money values may clearly be made upon *any* circumstances sure to recur. Having, then, before us, the probability of death in each year of age, we have only to charge each individual that sum which is the aggregate of the present values of the cost of insurance for each successive year of life, and we have what may be termed the *cost* of assurance. If one lives longer than those assured with him, he helps those who die early: if he dies early, they help him. In this way a perfect *average* is secured, which, being based on accurate and sufficient life-tables, is just as reliable as the equilibrium of the planets.

The deficient payments of those who die early are compensated for by the additional payments of those who live longer. Of course, to the actual *cost* of assurance, there must be added office and other expenses, use of capital, a surplusage for security, etc., and all these put together make up what are called the *rates* of assurance, rendering it safe to issue policies at these charges, whether for the whole term of life, or for a certain period, on the endowment plan.

The following, from the pen of an unknown writer, is a pretty lucid statement of the theory and practice of Life Assurance:

All Insurance is but the taking upon many the risk of one, so that if he loses what he insures they collectively shall make it good to him. If they be a thousand, his loss divided among so many hurts nobody; while if it had fallen upon one only it would have ruined him. Say, for example, that one thousand persons, at the age of thirty, assure each other for life to the amount of $1,000 each, and that each pays for this protection a yearly premium of $23.60. The collective premium will make $23,600. The casualties the first year will be probably eight, so that instead of the society having to pay back the whole $23,600 which they have received, they would have to pay back but $8,000. This will leave, with accrued interest at four per cent., $16,544 on their hands to meet subsequent losses, and this fund with future premiums, as fast as received, will be put out at interest. The next year sees the business renewed in favor of nine hundred and ninety-two survivors, of whom a like number will die during the second year, say eight persons. To the heirs of each of these again is paid $1,000, collectively $8,000. The third year sees nine hundred and eighty-four survivors whose premiums bring in $23,222. Once more, an increased number of these, or nine, die during the third year, and $9,000 is paid to their representatives. The fourth and each following year proceed in like manner until about the sixty-fifth year they will in nearly every case all have died, and a thousand times $1,000 will have been paid them; that is $1,000,000.

To the INDIVIDUAL, then, Life Assurance holds out PROTECTION; and to the CAPITALIST, the profit of taking those chances of life and death which the individual must not run, and can fairly pay to have lifted from his shoulders; as is the case when one takes advantage of fire or marine insurance.

THE PRACTICE ELUCIDATED.

REDUCING to practice the theory as explained in the foregoing chapter, there are a few points that may require further elucidation.

The *working plans* of companies differ. While all are based upon the same fundamental principles, they are organized upon different systems, and vary in the conditions adopted, and in the detail and application of benefits. Thus, there are joint-stock companies, strictly so called, in which a capital is furnished as security to the assured, by individuals who receive all the profit or surplus premiums of the business, as a remuneration for the risk and use of their capital. And the mixed, or part proprietary company and part mutual, having also a joint-stock guarantee capital, but allowing a portion of the profits, or *all* the profits, to policy-holders, after deducting legal interest upon the guarantee capital. And the purely mutual companies, in which all the surplus, or profits of the business, belongs to the policy-holders in proportion to the premium they pay. There are also companies in which the payments of policy-holders are wholly in cash, and others where partial payment is made in notes.

The matter of *profits, dividends, &c.*, may also require some explanation. If there was but one invariable rate of mortality from which we could determine the exact number of assured persons who would die at each age; if the rate of interest never fluctuated, and it could be precisely determined per policy what the expenses of management would be, the rate of premium deduced therefrom would be, as we have previously stated, the exact value of the sum assured. But as it is impossible to obtain an absolutely accurate rate of mortality, and also to prevent the admission of some bad lives, and as the interest of money is constantly varying, it is absolutely necessary, for the security of the assured, *to be certain* that the premiums charged are *sufficiently high* to cover the risks incurred. Hence, the rates are expected to be somewhat higher than will eventually prove to have been necessary. Here is an income or source of profit.

To this must be added several other sources of revenue. In calculating *interest* the rates are ASSUMED at 3 per cent. in England, and in this country at 4 per cent.; while a company, *in fact*, receives 6 or 7 per cent., often more. This is done by judicious investments, or loaning on good terms. These investments, of course, are drawing interest, which interest is again reloaned, making an investment at compound interest. These interests are an accumulation to the benefit of the company; which, in a few years, in a successful one, whose expenses are proportionate to their business, amounts to a large sum. Again, in order to cover expenses and still further to provide against all contingencies, the companies universally add to the rates obtained by calculation from correct tables of mortality, a loading of from 20 to 40 per cent. This is usually found more than is necessary, and forms another source of profit. Moreover, the lives which are assured are much better than the average of lives upon which the tables of mortality are based, the average expectancy being increased by the judicious selections made by the office; this consequently results in a profit. A profit is also acquired by the lapse, or loss, of policies from non-payment, and by the purchase of policies, as the company always reserve a sufficient amount to indemnify them for the risk already incurred.

In these several ways, and others incidental to the business, it happens that all companies managed with prudence, accumulate a larger amount of funds than is necessary to provide for future losses.

The adequacy of the premiums charged is tested by a "valuation" of the income and liabilities of the Society, which the offices make at certain periods, and if it results that they have a surplus after putting by sufficient to meet every probable claim upon them, they then distribute their profits. All profits in purely stock companies are divided among the stockholders; while in mutual and mixed companies they are distributed among the life members in an equitable proportion. In the distribution of surplus funds periods of three or five years have usually been preferred to shorter ones; because the rate of mortality is generally supposed to be more uniform among a large number of persons, and extending over a long period. Many companies in England, for this reason, make their dividends only once in seven or ten years. In some companies, however, both in England and America, the dividends are declared annually. The funds returned to the assured are generally disposed of as each may prefer; either to reduce the annual premium, or to the purchase of additional assurance without farther charge for premium (adding the dividend to the policy), or to abate the amount of future premiums, the sum assured remaining the same.

A few words may be in place as to the *lapse* or *surrender of policies.* It is sometimes complained by those wishing from any cause to withdraw from a company, that they do not get the full value of their policies.

Professor De Morgan observes on this, "Among the sources from which the offices draw profit, are lapsed policies. But what they receive by the lapse of the policy is not all profit; but only that portion by which the premium for the whole life exceeds the premium for a temporary assurance. Every premium which is paid by an assurer contains the consideration given for the chance of his dying in each and every subsequent year. If, then, he remain a member of the office and stand the risk of death during a certain number of years, all such part of his premiums as was consumed for the risk of those years become due to the office and was taken by the office as compensation for the risks, and cannot, therefore, be said to fall to them as profit upon the lapse of the policy. Two individuals, A and B, go to the office on the same day, and assure their lives for the same sum, A upon his whole life, and B for seven years. A pays, say £10 of premium, and B £7. At the end of seven years A allows his policy to lapse just at the time when B's policy expires by its own construction. What does the office gain by the lapse? Evidently, the temporary annuity of £3 by which the two premiums differ. The £7 paid by A out of £10 is not more than sufficient to pay his share of the claims which arose during the years which he continued in the office; the remaining £3 was a reserve for future years, which becomes profit to the office on his declining to stand the risks of these years."

This would seem to be sufficiently plain. The principle of assurance is, that the claims of those who die early are paid by the contributions of those who live long; therefore, if the *whole* of the premiums were returned to parties surrendering their policies, it might become impossible for an office to fulfill its engagements.

THE MORAL ASPECT OF LIFE OPERATIONS.

NO view could be more incorrect than that LIFE transactions are simply like other insurance transactions. They are of a far higher and more sacred character. They differ in these important respects.

Other kinds of insurance, for instance, pertain to *property* merely. A fire or marine insurance company deals simply with material objects—assumes risks upon houses, ships, merchandise. And then, again, its transactions are with one party. They begin and terminate with the insured.

Not so with a *Life* Company. Here the operations touch *human existence.* They relate to its fall or continuance. That for which one will "give all that he hath" is the matter bargained about. A man may *speculate* in *property*, but how abhorrent the idea of speculating in human life! A man may barter and banter where mere *goods* are concerned; but what a degradation to bring *life* operations down to this low level! A man may think lightly and speak flippantly of the destruction of barns and merchandise; but of the *end of earthly existence* he is expected to entertain a degree of seriousness.

Then, too, the Life office has to do with *other parties* than the assured. It is virtually acting for widows and orphans. It assumes to be their almoner and protector. A husband and father entrusts to it what is expected to mature only at his death. If there be fraud or unfairness, it is at once against the *dead and the living.* The wrong takes place when the party originally dealt with cannot set up a defense for the innocents; since he is no more one among them. And those for whom he toiled, and planned, and sacrificed, are now deprived at once of their just rights, and of the fruits of his efforts. Their sustenance is taken from before their mouths. The table is bare, where love, in anticipation, spread a bounteous repast. The guardians of the now defenseless ones have become their despoilers. How could there be a grosser wrong—a more aggravated wickedness?

Viewed in this light, how high the obligations which a Life office assumes! How sacred its trusts! And, consequently, *how honorable and how elevated should be its aims and operations!*

Now, an *agent* is expected to be the exponent of this moral dignity which ought to invest transactions in life. He is the *representative* of these transactions. Men form their ideas, not only of his particular Company, but of Life Assurance itself, from *him*. Any act of an Agent which is not honorable, has a direct tendency to dishonor himself and all his fellow-laborers. And not only this, it brings odium upon the whole institution. It poisons the system of Life Assurance, and works so much towards its ruin.

For these reasons, a Life Agent ought to be the very highest style of a man. What a fire, or marine, or banking or other agent may be, is nothing to him. *He* is to be much more than is expected of others. There is to be in him more of conscience; more of genuine goodness; more of the powers of honest persuasion; more of the capacity to appreciate and to use those motives which appeal to the higher and finer sensibilities.

And we earnestly maintain that Life Assurance will never realize its best capabilities, until it is practically elevated to the high moral position here assigned to it.

In the following chapter, the aim has been to analyze and set in order, and to inculcate the principal elements which constitute a permanently effective agency.

THE QUALITIES OF A GOOD AGENT.

1 HE APPRECIATES HIS WORK.

ONE can generally form a pretty accurate opinion of a Life Company by an acquaintance with its agents. The good agent understands and appreciates this fact, and also that men will judge of the whole system of Life Assurance by him. Accepting an appointment, therefore, he feels his responsibility. He has high ideas of his work. He looks upon it as benefiting the party assured, by giving to him quiet of mind; by inducing habits of economy, sobriety, and forethought; by setting before him an honorable motive to action and enterprise, and by leading him to the discharge of a sacred duty.

He considers that his efforts are helping to rid the community of poverty and its frequent attendants—vice and crime. And also that he is strengthening the sinews of social life by every policy he obtains. And what is more, that he is befriending the poor and needy; wiping sorrow from eyes dimmed with tears, and deserving the tribute of gratitude awarded to one of old: "When the ear heard me then it blessed me, and when the eye saw me it gave witness to me; because I delivered the poor that cried, and the fatherless, and him that had none to help him. The blessing of him that was ready to perish came upon me, and I caused the widow's heart to sing for joy."

An eminent minister once said: "Were I to leave the ministry, I should take an agency for Life Assurance; for I consider that it, next to direct religious efforts, is doing most to benefit society." And a very high authority—the Hon. ELIZUR WRIGHT, late Insurance Commissioner of Massachusetts—says: "Among the honorable workers in the civilized world, to whom the public as well as the assured will die indebted, we give *faithful and successful Life Assurance Agents a high place;* and no field that we know of is more inviting to an ambition that would devote the best of talent to the benefit of society at large, and individuals in particular."

To have such a conception of the value and dignity of an agent's vocation, is an important point gained. In such a case, where the motives of worldly policy are pleasantly mingled with higher moral considerations, and all these blend together in the beautiful philosophy which constitutes the chief charm of Life Assurance, the business of an agency will be both agreeable and successful. But *without* this appreciation of his work, how can an agent expect to succeed? How can he have faith in it, and impart to others confidence and interest in it? If he does not *appreciate* its benefits, how can he forcibly place them before others?

As a first thing, then, let an agent endeavor to rise up to a just estimate of the value and the moral grandeur of his undertaking. (See also, on this, page 43, etc.)

2. He is Moved by High Impulses.

A WRITER observes that some agents walk about like apprentices to an undertaker, proclaiming in sepulchral tones the uncertainty of life, &c., and they never succeed; while some of the jolliest fellows in existence are very successful agents, because they carry sound

3

and well-balanced minds, with a love of their fellow man, and can appreciate and feel the motives that will sway those with whom they come in contact.

We have seen men acting as agents, who seemed to feel that they were doing a mean sort of work, and needed to beg pardon of all creation for being about such work—for *being alive,* we had almost said,—whereas, they may well hold up their heads, and go out to their task animated by the very highest motives of philanthropy and moral obligation.

One should look upon his business in the light already presented, as a great public benefit, and feel that it does not detract from his being a promoter of the general good of mankind because he *gets a living by his labor.* He who does the state a service while at the same time earning an honest livelihood, is deserving of double honor, first because he promotes the public weal, and next because he secures his dependents against want.

Let a Life Agent, then, feel self-assured and confident. He need not depreciate his calling, as compared with any other business or profession whatever. Merchants, lawyers, physicians, school-teachers, secretaries and agents of benevolent societies even, are often doing less to scatter benefits throughout the human family, than are honest and efficient Life Agents. Far be it from them to feel that they are palming off something that is not worth what is paid as an equivalent, and infinitely more too. If not now, some time, blessings will be pronounced upon them.

3. His Heart is Enlisted.

OF a celebrated living actress, whose powers are worthy of a better cause, it has been written—

"We listening weep; but every burning drop
Flows from *thy heart*, ere falling from *our eyes*."

To make others feel, we must first *ourselves* feel. Deep conviction is contagious. It wins its way. It speaks in the eye, the looks, the tone. Other things being equal, a man's force in impressing others is in the ratio of his own *heart-force*. Says Goethe:

"*Persuasion*, friend, comes not by toil or art;
Hard study never made the matter clearer;
'*Tis the live fountain in the speaker's heart*
Sends forth the streams that melt the ravished hearer.
Would you, then, touch the heart, the only method known
My worthy friend, is *first to have one of your own.*"

All this applies well to a Life agent. If he *loves* his work; if he *puts his heart under it*, look out for results! To do much, he *must be full of it.* A Secretary once wrote to a newly-appointed agent: "Your very boots must creak the name of your Company!" It reminded us of the advice of Dr. J. W. Alexander to a ministering brother, as to having his heart enlisted in sermonizing: "Live for your sermon. Live in your sermon. Get some starling to cry—'Sermon! sermon!'"

No class of men ever propagated a great interest, and carried it through to victory, who did not first *wed* it, and wholly cast in their lot with it for better or for worse.

All effective agents have "Life Assurance on the brain." They spring to their task with an elastic and buoyant spirit. Write it down as a rule, that no man ever does much who is not enthusiastic in his profession or business—who does not think *his* enterprise, whatever it be, the greatest, or at least *one* of the greatest, and most important in the world. Only then are his energies untiring. Only then does the fire in his own soul kindle upon the souls of others.

4. HE IS ACTIVE AND INDUSTRIOUS.

WHEN a lady once asked Turner, the celebrated English painter, what his secret was, he replied: "I have no secret, madam, but hard work." This is a secret that many have never learned, and from this cause they don't succeed. Labor is the genius that changes the world from ugliness to beauty, and the greatest curse to one of the greatest blessing.

It is eminently true in Life Assurance, that "the hand of the diligent maketh rich:" while "idleness clotheth a man in rags."

There is no way of getting on well in a Life agency, short of absolutely *hard work*, and the *devotion of time* to it. The agent must be a man not only to 'strike the iron while it is hot,' but as Cromwell said, 'to make the iron hot by striking.' "*Peu et peu*,"—little by little—is a motto to be hung up in the agents' office. Or this: "Only work wins."

Luther was once asked how he found time to translate the Bible. His reply was, "I did a little every day." And Beethoven, when fifty-two years of age, wrote to his friend Wegeler, "My maxim has always been *nulla dies sine linea*—(no day without a line), and if I allow my muse to slumber, it is only that she may awake with fresh vigor."

A Life agent accepting such sentiments is on the road to success.

5. He is Courageous and Determined.

ONE should not accept a Life-agency until he has *made up his mind to succeed.* It has its difficulties and discouragements. But you must remember that a man can hardly be expected to jump into *any* splendid business at once. Very few agents are as successful as they could desire at the outset. One of the most efficient agents in the country worked diligently for six weeks before he took his first risk; but he said, "*I am bound to succeed.*" During the *next* three months his commissions were over twelve hundred dollars.

"The wise and active conquer difficulties
By *daring to attempt them*; sloth and folly
Shiver and sink at sights of toil and hazard,
And *make the impossibility they fear.*"

The old Crusaders used to say, "Faint heart never won fair lady." Another adage in everybody's mouth declares that "Fortune favors the brave."

That famous educator, Miss Mary Lyon, of South Hadley, Mass., used to say to her pupils, "If you commence teaching and do not succeed, *teach till you do succeed.*"

If the agent gets sorely disappointed in cases where he

was confident, let him nevertheless remember the lines in the *Loves of the Angels:*

"*Hope's* precious pearl in sorrow's cup
Unmelted at the bottom lay,
To shine again when, all drunk up,
The bitterness should pass away."

A newly-appointed agent once said, when finding it hard to get a start, and to make both ends meet in living, "I will share a dry cracker with my wife sooner than give it up!" We scarcely need add that he had a permanent success.

Here one may well write over his office-door General Grant's famous dispatch, "I will fight it on this line," etc. or the couplet of Sir Walter Scott:

"Come one, come all—this rock shall fly
From its firm base as soon as I."

Never, in a solitary case, have we known an agent to complain of a lack of business, if he patiently went at it with full faith that

"In the bright vocabulary of youth
There's no such word as FAIL!"

6. He has Tact and Discrimination.

THE great thing in assuring men is to use that particular argument at the right moment which will gain the object. Or, which is the same thing, to say just what will carry conviction and lead to immediate and conclusive action—and *nothing more.* Of some men in urging assurance it may be said,

> "——— His zeal
> None seconded, as *out of season* judged,
> Or *singular*, or *rash.*"

Some agents *presume too little.* Better take for granted that the man you approach *will* assure. Better assume that he *is ready*. Approach him saying, "Here is something for your interest; something you want; perhaps the best thing you ever met with." Tell him what it is, and act as if you *expected* him to close up the matter at once.

Some agents *talk too much.* Never is a flood of words more out of place than in urging Life Assurance. *Don't* talk the man to death! Let him have time to breathe, and breathe yourself. Watch the motions of the countenance. Trace the workings of the mind. Mark what pleases. If you have made a point, don't *un*make it. Now be cautious in speaking! One indiscreet remark just at this moment may be fatal to your purpose.

Some agents *explain too minutely.* They are too fearful—scrupulous, shall we say—lest the man shall not *see* everything about the whole subject. So they must *argue* and *demonstrate,* until the man's mind is confused, or rendered indifferent. Aim to persuade, to *move,* rather than to convince. Very likely he *believes* in assurance now. Address yourself to the one work of leading him on into it.

At a meeting of solicitors the question was once raised: "What tables do you find most popular?" One replied: "I never ask 'what table do you prefer?' I *tell him what table he wants,* and go about assuring him! I get out the application, and ask for his full name, and hold the pen to write it down; and so carry the man right along with me till the thing is completed!"

Oftentimes a bold move of this kind is most successful. In other cases things must proceed with greater deliberation. At any rate, don't commit the man if there is danger of a refusal. Don't hear it, if given; but leave the matter for some other time.

Let an agent, in these and other particulars, study human nature, and acquire tact and discrimination. If thoughtful and attentive, he will be sure to acquire it, and much more readily than he may imagine.

7. He Speaks the Truth.

"First in the glories of thy front
Let the crown-jewel TRUTH be found."

REQUESTING of an officer in a Life Company to name a subject for an article to agents, he said, "Write on this: *How to get along without lying.*" And he added, "Agents will lie!—they tell anything that suits their purpose—and this gives a bad name to the whole business." Certainly this is far from being true of all agents, but it is true of too many.

It is high time that Life Agents set their faces against this practice of deception. They may rest assured that here, as everywhere, "honesty is the best policy."

"A man of sense will artifice disdain,
As men of wealth may venture to go plain."

In the end misrepresentations are pretty sure to be visited upon the offender's own head; so that

"They that act unjustly
Are the worst rebels to themselves."

And how abhorrent the idea of trifling with the confidence of men, and so misleading and deceiving them that they shall hereafter say: "He is dishonest; I would not believe him under oath;" as one was lately heard to say of an agent who had told him what proved to be untrue in respect to his premiums and dividends.

Benjamin Franklin is often quoted as authority for the value of Life Assurance, and very properly so. But Franklin said, "*Let honesty be as the breath of thy soul.*"

8. He has a Good Reputation.

OF an agent's *veracity* men ought not only to be able to affirm,

"——— What he says
You may believe, and pawn your soul upon it;"

but they ought to be able to compliment him throughout as a thoroughly honest and true man.

The remark has been made by somebody, concerning writers, that "*it makes all the difference in the world who is behind the pen.*" If we know that a writer or speaker is tricky, scheming, hypocritical, or corrupt, we refuse to be influenced by him. On the other hand, it is remarkable what weight the words of a man of character have.

All this is equally true in business success. And hence the reputation of an agent in the community should be unequivocally good. It will be found a ehief element of strength. Let him aim to be an *honor* to the Company he represents remembering that *it* will be judged of by *him*, and that he should do nothing to derogate from its good name, or from the reputation of Life Assurance in general. Let him be strictly temperate, and in all respects so bear himself that even his opponents will be compelled to say,

"I've scanned the actions of his daily life
With all the industrious malice of a foe,
And nothing meets mine eyes but deeds of honor."

9. He is Agreeable in Manners.

TREATING everybody in a respectful way, is one of the surest means of getting on in the world. It costs but little, and is worth a great deal. A buffoon,

"Fit for the mountains and the barbarous caves,
Where manners ne'er were preached,"

is out of place in a Life Agency. Coarseness, vulgarity, looseness of conversation, repulsive manners—all this is disgraceful, and a serious drawback upon success.

So honorable and beneficent is the vocation of a Life Agent, that we instinctively demand in him a correspondence to the portraiture,

"Tho' modest, on his unembarrassed brow
Nature had written 'GENTLEMAN.'"

We demand that he shall be

"—For courtesy, behavicr, language,
And every fair demeanor, an example."

The pen-picture of a quaint writer, sketching the *true gentleman*, is worthy of the study of a Life Agent:

"He is above a low thing. He cannot stoop to a mean fraud. He invades no secret in the keeping of another. He betrays no secrets confided to his own keeping. He never struts in borrowed plumage. He never takes selfish advantage of one's mistakes. He uses no ignoble weapons in controversy. He never stabs in the dark. He is ashamed of inuendoes. He is not one thing to a man's face, and another behind his back. He may be trusted out of sight —near the thinnest partition—anywhere He buys no offices, he sells none, he intrigues for none. He would rather fail of his rights than win them through dishonor. He will eat honest bread. He tramples on no sensitive feeling. He insults no man. If he have rebuke for another he is straightforward, open, manly. He cannot descend to scurrility. In short, whatever he judges honorable he practices toward every man." To such gentlemanly bearings as this, large tolerance will be yielded, even under the most persistent urgency.

10. He is Devoted to his Calling.

LIVE MEN are nowhere more needed than in Assurance Agencies. They are a *necessity* in a community, and probably always will be, because men *will not spontaneously go into Assurance.* Instruction, persuasion, reminding them of an imperative duty, is essential. Here is room for the perpetual play of an agent's best powers. Unless he *stir up* men, a great obligation is passed by unnoticed. *There is no adequate substitute for activity among assurance agents.* The public is practically incapable of performing its duties without the continual urgency of individuals whose interest it is to importune men to do themselves justice. And it is surprising how much a few energetic minds—*one* energetic mind, even—may do towards informing and exciting the public on this subject.

Agents often distrust their ability to succeed in the business of Life assurance to such an extent as will warrant them in devoting their whole time to it, and so they make small gains by other means. But the lesson of experience is, that in order to succeed, all the tact, ability, and energy must be concentrated on *this one work.*

The *essential* thing is that the agent be *absorbed in his vocation.* The largest powers become weak when divided and dissipated among many aims. Inferior powers are mighty when concentrated. It is very seldom that a man does different things *well.* Life agents who have rolled up for themselves a splendid income, have not done it by carrying on other matters at the same time. They took up Life Assurance as a *business for life;* and they *prosecuted it with singleness of aim, and an absolute concentration of their best faculties.*

11. His Interest is in One Company.

UNLESS it is specially understood at the time an agent receives his appointment that he has liberty to solicit applications for other companies, *it is expected that he will work exclusively for the company appointing him.* The reason is plain. No agent can do full justice to any one company when he is equally interested in advocating the claims of one or two more. He should have HIS *preferences* in order to make others have *theirs.* And the loose, scattering way of offering one thing or another with equal recommendation, is injurious to all parties. A high authority remarks, that "however it may appear to a novice in the business, it is the uniform testimony of agents who have had large experience in Life Assurance, that it is far best to bring all the ability and enthusiasm one can command to the advocacy of the claims of a *single company.*"

12. Careful in Selecting Risks.

IT cannot be too deeply impressed upon the mind of an agent, that poor risks are a damage both to himself and to the company. The officers watch the *losses* as closely as they do the business of the agent. Some men secure a large number of policies, and at the same time are careless as to the selection of the risks; and the result is that the ratio of the losses through that agent exceed that of the *average* ratio of the company's risks; and so in the end he is dismissed in digrace, and loses the benefit of his labors, and also his position as a life agent; while those who have done a much smaller business, and done it carefully, are strengthened in the confidence of the company, and permanently retained. One loss in your new field may more than counterbalance the profits of your agency for a year In every way show to the Company that they can *rely upon your judgment.*

BEGINNING THE BUSINESS.

1. Personal Canvass at the Outset.

BEFORE one can become a successful manager of a Life Agency, he must have had *actual work in getting applications.* This is beginning at the bottom. Nothing can compensate for the lack of this lesson at the feet of that best teacher, Experience.

A beginner in the business must therefore begin *here.* He will in this way learn more in a few days than he would in weeks of theorizing. Let him take right hold of canvassing, without stopping for anything. Let him try his hand at it, and learn how to use his tools *by using them.* If you are timid, doubtful, *strike out!*

"Tender-handed stroke the nettle,
And it stings you for your pains;
Grasp it like a man of mettle,
And it soft as silk remains."

And remember the saying of a French author: "*It is the first step that costs.*" That is the difficult one. Take that; take it rightly, and half the trouble in starting business is got along with.

2. A Policy on his Own Life.

A CIVIL engineer once had finished a complicated railroad bridge, when many speculated and doubted as to its strength. Mounting a huge engine, he ordered it out upon the bridge, and crossed and recrossed at full speed. He thus gave proof of his faith in his own structure.

A Life agent is expected to do likewise. If asked "Are *you* assured in this Company?" it would be a sorry answer if obliged to say "no!" But if he can say "yes," it will act as an inducement to others. And all the better if he can say "I have a *large* policy;" naming a heavy amount.

It should be added, that your taking a policy on your own life is evidence to the Company of sincere earnestness in accepting an agency.

It is also an excellent habit to carry your policy, (as well as a list of large policyholders and the sums they are assured for,) in your pocket, and show it on suitable occasions, pointing out its provisions and advantages.

3. Familiarity With Life Assurance.

LEISURE hours should now be employed in "reading one's self up" as to Life Assurance:—its origin, history, science, and a thousand other facts and particulars. Reports of 'Commissioners' are valuable. A monthly Assurance Journal will be found stimulating and rewarding. An agent should not be a novice. If he shows familiarity with his business it gives other persons confidence in the Company he represents. Then, too, one perfectly familiar with his business, and the relations which exist between the *assurer* and *assured*, has the power to enforce the advantages of the whole system of Life Assurance to the conviction of his friends in a manner at once agreeable and pertinent. It requires no great power of persuasion to induce people of ordinary prudence to insure their *property* against destruction by *fire* or *water*, but it *does* require some power of persuasion, and appropriateness of illustration, to induce one to take a *life* policy.

Hence, if one would be master of his business, he must be a round-about, full, broad-minded, and ready man.

4. Posted as to his Company.

IT is especially necessary that an agent understand all about the Company he represents. Its *strong points* should be appreciated, and kept prominent. We know agents who say very little, but come right to the *special advantages* offered by their Company, and generally carry their case.

Where objection is made that in this or that particular some *other* company surpasses yours in advantages, the agent must be able to give *facts*. Hence, he should *know*, and be ready to *produce* whatever considerations will relieve the apparent difficulty or objection. From this it will be seen how important it is to be thoroughly posted on the *comparative merits* of his own and other companies.

5. His Medical Examiner.

WHERE the agent has the selection of his medical examiner, one of undoubted skill and soundness of judgment should first of all be sought. If to this be added agreeable manners, and a pleasant way of approaching and handling men, rather than a brusque, cold, repulsive way, as is sometimes the case, it will be a valuable qualification; for the bearing of the medical examiner has a great deal to do with making it pleasant for applicants.

The agent should also, if possible, induce the physician to take a policy in the office employing him. And where this is not possible, he should use every endeavor to *interest the examiner in the success of the agency, and secure his influence and co-operation.* In many cases, the consulting physician will give the agent *a list of his patrons,* and his card as an introduction. It is a great point gained if the doctor be thus enlisted as your helper.

Get the medical examination made *at once* after obtaining each proposal. See that your doctor attends to it without delay.

6. Acquaintances Registered and Visited.

SOON as a start is thus obtained, the agent should make out a complete list of all his friends and acquaintances, and set about the work of seeing and addressing them personally:— perhaps sometimes sending, in advance, a card, circular, or office-book. He should not overlook or neglect doubtful cases, for the most unlikely are often the first to assure. He should count no visit lost. Where it is not convenient for the party to give you a hearing now, the interview had better be deferred. There is no use in pressing the matter upon a man's attention when his head is full of something else, or when he is in a hurry, or in bad humor. There may be persistence without giving offense, or provoking a rebuff. And however coldly received, or even insulted, bear it, and when it comes around right, try it again. By all means, never allow yourself to be annoyed; keep your temper on all occasions, and at all times "learn to labor and to wait." Always endeavor to leave a good impression. It will be of value to you at some future time.

7. Making New Acquaintances.

PERSONAL acquaintance with men is your great *stock in trade.* By every suitable means this should be extended. If starting business in a city or village where you are not generally acquainted, it will be well to turn to the banks, public societies, companies, and associations of various kinds, as found advertised or registered in the fly-leaves of the *Directory*, and thus ascertain the *leading men of the place.* Make out a list of those you do not know, and seek means and opportunities of favorable introductions to them. In time, you may approach almost every one of them. It is an advantage, also, to belong to literary and other societies.

8. GETTING NAMES FOR REFERENCE.

A BOARD of local references can in most cases be readily obtained. But it is of great importance to secure the best known and most respectable citizens. You can frankly state to such that it would be an advantage to have the use of their names, and that you would like to be able to say they are assured in your company. This will be a motive that you can use in soliciting them to take a policy. Those to whom you refer should, if possible, be policy-holders in the company. In very rare cases (of highly distinguished persons) this rule may be departed from.

But, whether holding policies in the company, or not, those to whom you refer should be carefully informed of the peculiarities of the company, and enlisted in its behalf.

To gain this point in respect to a particular individual is often worth any amount of effort.

9. TREATMENT OF OTHER AGENTS.

THERE can be no reason why agents of different companies residing in the same town should not, as a rule, be on good terms with each other. At any rate there should be no discourtesy between them, and all attempts to procure business by depreciation of other agents and companies will generally be to the detractor's disadvantage. Excepting where the unworthiness of a company, or its agent, is notorious, insinuations as to its being in "a dangerous condition," and its officers being "unworthy to be trusted," and the like, prove an injury to Life Assurance generally, and, to say the least, are of doubtful temporary advantage. It is generally sufficient to show the excellencies of your own company.

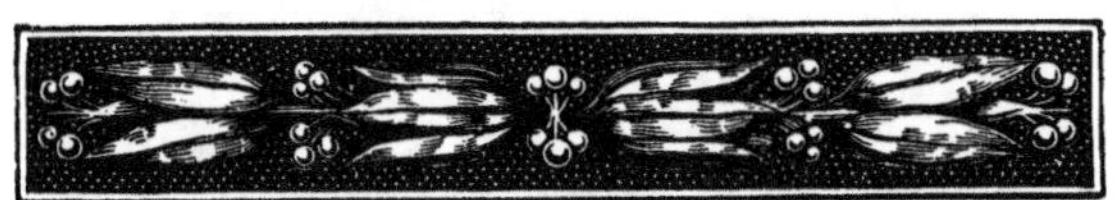

MANAGING THE BUSINESS.

1. ORDER AND METHOD IN EVERYTHING.

LET the agent keep in mind that "order is heaven's first law." In the office there should be "a place for everything and everything in its place." A slovenly appearance in the office is indicative of careless habits generally.

An agent's books should be systematized and well posted, so that he can turn to any point in a moment. Every possible fact should there be properly recorded; such as his accounts with the company, and with each policyholder, and the residence, &c., &c., of the latter.

And it is very desirable to devote a *particular part of each day,* regularly, to *canvassing. Without* this one *may* do business; *with* it, he *must* do it.

2. Relations to the Home Office.

EVERY good agent will feel a pleasure in acquiescing with the Company's rules and regulations respecting agencies. He will be prompt and regular in all reports and remittances. He will be frank and honorable, eschewing all double-dealing, secret negotiations with other companies while he is supposed to be acting in good faith for his own, and the like. He will write to the President, or General Agent, *confidentially,* and show in every way that he has the company's interest at heart. Whatever affects the company's standing or success, he considers as affecting him. He feels closely identified with it, and therefore works for it with a zest. If the least misunderstanding arises, he is quick to have it explained and made right. At the same time, if there be any points connected with the business that he does not clearly comprehend—such, for instance, as the various methods of assurance offered, the mode of dividing profits, etc., he does not remain in doubt, but writes at once for information.

3. SATISFIED WITH TERMS.

SOME agents are given to perpetual uneasiness as to terms, and better chances, etc. But it should not be forgotten, that what is for the *agent's* interest is for the *company's* interest; and that therefore it is to be presumed that a company will deal liberally with its agents. Whatever is reasonable will be pretty sure to be granted.

And an agent may settle this in his mind: that *whatever he is worth he will in the end fetch.* If he proves himself worthy of a better chance, he will be sure to get it. The thing for him to do, then, is to *show that he can do Life business.* This is the *only* thing he need concern himself about at the outset. He only asks a foothold—a chance to demonstrate that he has capacity for *this work.* If it is in him it will be sure to come out; and he will soon find his level and get as good a position somewhere as he deserves. Two lines in Addison's *Cato* may well be remembered:

"'Tis not in mortals to *command* success;
But we'll *do more,* Sempronius—*we'll deserve it!*"

4. Prompt Delivery of Policies.

THE delivery of policies should be made as soon as possible after they come into the hands of an agent. Delay may bring a change of mind on the part of an applicant. A large proportion of returned policies would have been taken if agents had promptly and personally attended to their business.

5. Renewals and Rejections.

WHEN a payment is to be made upon a policy, it affords an opportunity for the agent to congratulate the assured upon his good investment; to inquire if he does not wish to increase the amount, and if he cannot name some of his friends who might desire to take out policies.

Where a party is rejected from want of sufficiently good health, it is well to ease over the disappointment as far as possible; to advise that he see the medical examiner some other time; and to express the hope that he will yet be able to forward a good application.

6. Helping the Hesitating.

YOU will come in contact with many men who never can *decide* to assure. They are convinced, and *all but* ready to act. But unless helped, they will never "cross the Rubicon." In such a case, get out your forms of proposal, ask for pen and ink, (or, better still, carry a portable ink-stand with you,) and commence filling up the form by asking the full name, etc., etc. An experienced agent remarks that you will find that nineteen men out of twenty will allow you to decide for them that which they would delay for months, or even years, if left to decide it for themselves. At the same time, with *some* men it will not do thus to assume that they are ready. You must wait their motion.

7. Filling out Applications.

READ carefully the directions printed on the margins of the application, or elsewhere, as to particulars, and write out the applications with extreme care, as this application *is the basis of a contract* upon which possibly widows and orphans may depend for their *all.* You have no right to peril it by haste or carelessness; or to subject the Company and yourself to delays and annoyances from the same cause.

In filling out the application, write replies to every question distinctly. Insert the full Christian name, both of the applicant and of the person whose life is to be assured.

The *signatures* must always be the ***full*** Christian names. All incomplete and incorrect applications will be returned to you.

8. Resign if Doing Nothing.

COMPLAINTS are often made by companies, that agents who do little or nothing do not throw up their commissions. It is but fair that an appointee either discharge the duties of his office, or vacate it in favor of another. Otherwise, important ground will be unoccupied, and the company will suffer harm from the impression which men get that it is doing no business.

A dead agency is worse than none. When a live man subsequently takes hold of it, he finds its antecedents a serious obstacle. He had a thousand times rather begin anew.

The moment, then, that the agent becomes satisfied that he cannot successfully fill the place, he should signify it to the Company.

ENLARGING THE BUSINESS.

1. WIDENING ONE'S FIELD.

UPON hearing a minister complain that his "field was too narrow," a brother replied, "*Then why don't you enlarge it?*" Better advice could not have been had. The same counsel might with profit be given to many a man occupying a Life agency which he deems "too contracted." On that same field some other man might be reaping a splendid harvest.

It is all a mistake (we speak as a general rule) to imagine that nothing can be done in a given place because there are "too many companies operating there," or "the people are pretty much all assured," or there is "too little money in circulation;" or something like it. In one sense, the more companies the better. The mind of the community will likely be stirred up to the matter of assurance, which is an important consideration.

The more people *know* of this subject the more they will like it. Life Assurance will one day be as common as fire insurance; and you may just as well think of exhausting or overdoing the one as the other. We had rather go into a community where there are a dozen companies, than where an agent had never been, and Life Assurance was wholly a new thing. In fine, no matter what the character of the field is, well directed effort will produce satisfactory results. It is not so much the *field* as the *man.*

2. STRIKING FOR LARGE POLICIES.

MANY agents err in not aiming high enough when soliciting policies. It is usually well to name a large sum, even if it be rejected. It will help to expand one's ideas, and secure him for a respectable amount.

And again, it is a great mistake to pass by the rich, and be always working at men with small means. "Nothing venture, nothing have." Try that man of independent means. Don't be afraid! If you secure *him*, it will make up for many failures. Remember that one policy of ten thousand dollars is worth *ten* policies of a thousand dollars.

Besides this, it gives standing to your company to identify with it those who are in affluent circumstances.

3. DEPENDING ON "MACHINERY."

IT is a trite remark of some one, that "the best way to do a thing is to *do* it!" While some men are *getting ready* to work, and "operating" their machinery, others will step in and accomplish the same thing without anybody's knowing it. An English writer says: "there are two kinds of agents. Some of them mean well, yet they think they must have a very large amount of stationery, and plates on their doors, and boards on houses, and large bills to stick about the town, and they are constantly asking for something of this kind. On the other hand, there is another class of agents who do little of this sort of thing. They remind us very much of the owners of two barges which got aground near London Bridge. One of them got a large number of horses, and brought all their strength to bear upon one of the barges, and tore it to pieces; the other watched for the tide, and when it rose seized the opportunity, and took it safely, with sails and helm, into harbor. Now, what we want agents to do is to seize opportunities, seek for them, and when they find them, not to make a great noise, but do the work right up." While one agent may be puffing his office in every newspaper in his neighborhood from year to year, the *working* agent is steadily and noiselessly accumulating a large business.

4. Editorial Notices.

AND yet we would by no means despise helps and auxiliaries in getting business. One of these is local (and if possible *editoral*) notices in the papers. It is very rare that this cannot be brought about; if not directly, then through the influence of other parties. One good editorial notice is worth a year's advertisement in the business columns. *By all means induce the editor to take a policy,* if the thing is possible, so that he can say "We are assured in this Company."

5. Use of Office-Books, etc.

JUDICIOUS distributions of these is desirable. If the Company is wholly unknown in the community, show-cards, circulars, office-books, annual statements, &c., may be freely given away. In many cases, however, in getting an application, no reading matter will be serviceable. We know agents who, as a rule, just take the tables of the Company in their hands and go out and get business—very rarely using any other printed matter. But where one *will* "think about it," it is wise to give him something to read, especially if it explains and enforces the assurance of life. So far as documents of any kind are really effective, they are a cheap investment. And they should be put into the hands of those already assured, as well as the unassured. This will increase their confidence, and in many cases they will show them to their friends.

6. Influence of the Minister.

LIFE agents should cultivate the acquaintance of the clergy, and by every suitable means endeavor to secure their influence. In most cases a minister will give a note of introduction, or a general letter commendatory of the agent and his Company. Often, too, a pastor will furnish a list of the members of his parish most likely to assure.

It is of great importance to effect an assurance upon the minister's life. Where he is unable, or disinclined, some one of his parishioners may be induced to take up the matter and raise the premium, and make a *present* to the pastor of a policy. Suggest this to some one of the members.

7. Sunday-School Teachers.

BECOMING associated with the Sunday-school will not only extend one's usefulness in general, but enhance his success as an agent. It gives him a standing in the community, introduces him to young men of enterprise and growing influence, and identifies him with the congregation and its leader.

8. Profiting by Deaths of Assured.

WHERE a life falls in the community with an assurance upon it, especially if it is of great advantage to the surviving members of the family, particulars may be profitably obtained, and the circumstances commented upon. Perhaps the relatives and friends may be induced to assure.

9. Same of the Unassured.

VERY few communities do not furnish examples where a life policy upon the deceased parent would have been a God-send to the afflicted household. It is not only proper to refer to such cases, but an agent is derelict in duty if he does not interpret and apply such providences as a warning against the neglect of Life Assurance. *Sudden* deaths give especial point to such appeals.

10. New Attention to Canvassing.

THE memorandum book may now be profitably re-filled with names of friends, and names of those whose acquaintance may be cultivated. It is ever to be borne in mind, that *personal canvass* is the one sure clue to a growing success. All other means put together will not amount to so much as the single matter of intelligent activity. Indeed, unless backed by activity they are of no avail. That which pays, and pays with compound interest, is the *direct grapple of the agent's mind upon the individual minds of the community.*

Write this down as an axiom: "ASSURANCE WILL NOT COME INTO MY OFFICE; I MUST GO OUT AND INVITE IT IN; I MUST, I WILL, SOLICIT, SOLICIT, SOLICIT!"

11. THE MOTIVE OF PATRONAGE.

A SHREWD agent will make every business relation tell upon his assurance business. The merchant, the mechanic, the banker, the physician, the grocer, the tailor, the printer, may reasonably be solicited to take a policy on the consideration of your patronage. If approached in a delicate way, no man will think the less of you for suggesting this. It is a fair business transaction.

12. NEVER WITHOUT BLANK APPLICATIONS.

THE hunter does not go into the woods and fields without ammunition. Neither should the Life agent cross the threshold of his office without being in a condition to "produce the documents," in case they are wanted. The neglect of this simple precaution has lost many an agent more than one application. While going for the gun the game fled! Be always ready to say, "Well, *let us fix it right up now! There's no time like the present!*"

13. Recommending New Agents.

IT is expected of an agent to keep an eye out for stirring business-men, adapted to a Life agency, who might like to change their occupation. These he will recommend to the Home Office for appointment, in case they are wanted either in his own or some other field. If he meets with agents of other companies who *desire* to dissolve their present connection, it is proper to mention it; but it is not honorable to try to induce them to change companies.

14. Operating through "Bosses," etc.

IN large business or manufacturing establishments, it is important to get the good-will of the principal head (and assure him if possible), and so obtain favorable access to those in his employ. Very often, also, the superintendent or foreman of a concern is a more useful friend than even the principal. Or one of the clerks or common workmen may, by proper influences, become of very great advantage in introducing the agent to his associates in the shop or the warehouse.

15. Soliciting the "Intimate Friend."

THIS is a most favorable way of introducing the subject of assurance; and the fact that a particular acquaintance has obtained a life policy, will often be a sufficient inducement for him at least to look into the subject of assurance. At the same time, he will naturally think well of the company to which his friend has given the preference. When practicable, get those about to be assured to go with you to their friends, introducing you, and commending to them Life Assurance, and the company you represent. This has great weight.

16. Convincing the Wives.

OFTENTIMES women are less favorable to Life Assurance than men. Many a wife absolutely *opposes* the husband's getting a policy. And others are indifferent to it, and, at least, do not press the matter till it is accomplished. It will be well to remind such wives that multitudes of their number are suffering to-day from this *indifference*, or *opposition*, or, perhaps, *foolish superstition*; that multitudes will be sorry for it *but once*, and that is, *always*. At the same time, urge the tender motive of *love to their children*.

17. Looking after the Newly-Married.

WE lately heard a sensible newly-married husband say, that from the time of his marriage until he placed an endowment life-policy of $5,000 in his desk, he had not drawn a free breath. He felt how totally destitute his wife would be, in case of his death; and he saw no way of meeting his obligation to provide for her support (which he had solemnly *pledged himself to do*), except by means of Life Assurance. When *this* was effected, he felt easy. Using such an example, an agent, calling on the newly-married, may also suggest how admirable a *present* to a bride a handsome life-policy would be. It will be well to precede the call by sending documents, showing the imperative duty of every married man to assure. Make the acquaintance of those about to marry, before the consummation of the event; this will render your chance a better one.

18. Making Each Assured a Helper.

IF he be wise in enlarging his business, an agent will be particular to enlist in his interest, so far as he can, erery one who takes a policy. In some cases, a slight compensation may ensure effort in this direction. But in other cases the offer of this would have a contrary effect. Here is room for wisdom and good sense. But it is highly desirable that an agent have numerous influences around him silently operating to his advantage.

19. Applying to Those Already Assured.

WITH some agents it is enough to find that one is already assured. How much better to congratulate him, and ask, "Would you not like to increase the amount?" and if for *life*, propose an *endowment* policy.

ARGUMENTS IN URGING ASSURANCE.

PRECISELY the motive to be urged in a given case, cannot, of course, with certainty, be specified. Each agent must choose and use his own special argument. We know agents who very seldom use more than one, e. g., that of an *investment*. Others make the *endowment* feature a specialty. A wise agent will soon see which motive is most effective, and in the main use that. Business arguments will, as a rule, effect far more than sentimental arguments. The argument that *tells* may, in many individual instances, be a very weak one in itself, but if it answers the purpose, it is everything. The illustration used may be homely, but if it effects its object it is superior to the most elegant metaphor. Confine yourself to a few strong points, and always present them in words so clear that any one can understand them.

We enumerate a variety of considerations, all of which are fair and legitimate motives in urging to action.

1. Scripture and Duty.

SCRIPTURE declares, "If any man provide not for his own, especially those of his own house, he hath denied the faith and is worse than an infidel." And this provision obviously should be made to extend (as it may by Life Assurance), beyond the possible fall of the parent's own life. It is not enough to feed his household daily while living. So far as he can do it, he is bound to see that a table is spread for them when he may no more sit beside it. *Just then* may they *most need* this provision.

2. Immediate Provision.

PROVISION for one's dependents should, obviously, be *immediate.* The old-fashioned slow way of "laying up something for a rainy day," has proved itself (alas, too often), wholly defective. Death does not wait for these slow accumulations. Not one in ten thousand, in the old way, lays by a competence for his family.

3. It is Found Here.

LIFE assurance *is an immediate provision.* It secures a fortune *instantly.* The moment a policy is made out and executed, *that moment* the family is secure against the worst of ills. You may die the next hour, but a fund *beyond all question* will come to their relief.

4. The Only Method Known.

ASSURANCE of life is the *only* immediate provision. In this respect it *stands alone.* Prof. E. WRIGHT, of Massachusetts, truly remarks that "LIFE ASSURANCE possesses EXCLUSIVELY the power of creating AT ONCE an adequate provision against the destitution of dependents in case of death." Therefore, *no other mode of accumulation is equal to this.*

5. UNCERTAINTY OF LIFE.

THE risk from the uncertainty of life may be urged. Refer to examples, and to the statistics of sudden deaths. Urge that one *knows* this—must *admit* it; and should *act* on it. Put the case thus: "The chance of your dying within the year is two per cent., while the chance that your dwelling will burn within the year is less than a quarter of one per cent. There are, therefore, EIGHT CHANCES THAT YOU WILL DIE WITHIN A WEEK to ONE THAT YOUR HOUSE WILL BURN within the same time; yet you will hasten on the wings of the wind to insure the latter, and fold your arms with perfect indifference to the former!"

6. POSSIBILITY OF SICKNESS.

MENTION the possibility of sickness, making it impossible to get a policy. Specify cases. Urge immediate action lest it be lamented when it is too late. "When the cold shiver runs through the frame, and the fevered tongue, and the short cough appear, it is TOO LATE to rush to the assurance office and offer yourself for examination!"

7. Family Affection.

AFFECTION to one's family is a strong motive. Find out particulars as to the wife, or children, and appeal to the wish to please them and do them good. You may often appeal on the ground of love for a dear *child.* The *father's* heart is tender, though the *man* be made of stone. The appeal may run thus:

"Would you not at this moment make sure a patrimony to your wife, or child, if you could? The instrument is within your reach! It is a Life-Policy!"

8. A Social Obligation.

IT is a political and social duty to assure. Refer to its influence upon social life; the solidity it imparts to all institutions; and the protection it affords to industry and labor. Besides this, no person has a right to expose his family to the necessity of public support. It is a wrong to the public. By this means, too, one can be in a condition to have his *debts paid,* which he is solemnly bound to do.

9. Its Beneficence.

HERE is a way to do good. Allude to the relief it pours so abundantly upon the bereaved and suffering, and to the countless benefits it scatters along the pathway of human life. Show that by this means pauperism and its frequent consequence, crime, are greatly lessened; and that genteel pauperism (the most cruel form in which the evil appears), can be entirely removed.

10. A Means of Self-Protection.

LIFE Assurance has two features:—beneficence and self-protection. As to the latter, it is found in an *endowment* policy: by which one secures a certain sum to be paid to himself at a given age, if he live to that age, or if he die earlier, to be paid when he dies, to his heirs. In this way provision is made for a time when one's energies fail, and he may need money rather than be called upon to pay it out, as on a life-policy. Said an old merchant who failed in 1861: "Had I taken an endowment policy thirty years ago I should not have felt the premiums from year to year, and I should have saved something to support me in my old age, *which I could do in no other way.*"

Urge that hundreds of our best business men are now practically showing their appreciation of this form of life assurance.

11. VARIETY OF USES.

THE uses and advantages of a life-policy may be presented as a motive. The case may be put thus:

"How convenient for an honest young man, for instance, to turn over a life-policy as security for money which he loans, and which he is sure to pay back IF HE LIVES. Creditors can assure the lives of their debtors, as a security for their claims. A man with incumbrances upon his property may assure to the amount of them, to secure their ready payment at the expiration of his term policy, or at his decease. A young man may raise money to complete his education, or to buy a stock of goods, or tools, or a farm, by assuring his life and assigning the policy as contingent security:" and the like.

12. A Good Investment.

VERY few investments are as profitable as this. Show that many wealthy men are going into Life Assurance merely because it is a good operation They say, "It is the best investment we can make: for in fact it combines the advantages of a Life Assurance, a Savings' Bank, and a safe Investment." Some of them are carrying policies for $25,000, $50,000, $100,000; and one man is known to be assured to the amount of $250,000. These are among our shrewdest business-men. Show, also, how many a valuable business has been sacrificed by the inability of a widow to wait until a fair price could be obtained, owing to ready money being required. If a merchant, show how valuable a policy becomes at a time of pressure as collateral security. And how, in a long lifetime, it becomes an investment paying a reasonable percentage for capital. And, also, how he can provide for his old age and for his family at the same time, by taking an endowment policy. If he is a member of a firm, point out the value of a provision paid from the business funds on the first of two or three lives, thus securing a safe portion for the widow of the first deceased partner without crippling the concern for those who shall be the survivors.

13. Increases Credit.

IT increases one's credit and adds to his business reputation. Reputation is money; and it is a mark of foresight, large-mindedness, and economy to assure. A merchant once advertised for a clerk. Out of two hundred applicants for the place, he was influenced in favor of a particular one by the young man's statement that he had kept a life-policy in force for five years.

14. Personal Advantage.

SHOW that it develops the amiable and generous traits of character; accustoms a man to think for others; induces habits of industry, economy, and accumulation; and, by relieving the mind from anxiety and over-exertion, promotes health and longevity. And then, what a comfort in "the last of earth." How soothing and sustaining the reflection that an ample life-policy will insure the bereaved family against want. Well has a high authority remarked, that, if we gauge the suffering of one manly heart, for that single hour when the films of death are curtaining his loved ones out of sight unprovided for, and remember how many such agonies Life Assurance has prevented, putting happy and hopeful farewells in their stead, after prolonging life, perhaps, by lightening care, we shall be ready to justify the companies in any necessary expense.

15. JOY TO THE HOUSEHOLD.

EXPLAIN how the whole family feels the sweet influence of Life Assurance. The *daughter* will not have to be kept from school to sew for a living. The *son* can get an education, or be set up in business. And even the group of *little ones* are more blithesome because papa has had recourse to the philosopher's stone that creates a capital in an instant. The *wife* rejoices in the calm reflection that God has opened to her and the children an effectual door of relief in case their natural protector and support is snatched away. And the *husband* feels that a load is off his mind. He is a new man. He has done his duty and has a right to trust God and be at peace.

16. A DICTATE OF PRUDENCE.

SIMPLE prudence demands it. Doubtless one reason why mortality is regulated by a law, is, that we might provide against some of the worst calamities attending it.

It is simply wicked to disregard such provisions; just as if sewerage, disinfective agencies, vaccination, lightning-rods, &c., were not used to prevent fevers, cholera, small-pox and destruction by lightning. It were neglecting a providential means of security. So here. And the time is sure to come, if it is not here already, when a man will be deemed just as imprudent to leave his life unassured as to neglect insuring his property. And just as severe censure will be visited in either case.

17. Final Appeal.

WHEN you have convinced the judgment, gather up all your powers to move the will. Grapple on to the man. Throw your soul into his soul, your will into his will. Kindly, but firmly, make him answer to his own conscience such questions as these:

"HAVE I DONE MY DUTY TO MY FAMILY? Have I done it to the FULL EXTENT OF MY PRESENT ABILITY? If I were to die to-night, would those who are dear to me be safe from the pangs of want? Would my children have a comfortable home and means of education? Would my wife be independent of the cold charities of the world? Would my estate pay my debts and leave a competency to my family?

If not, must I not obtain a life-policy before I sleep, and so substitute the CERTAINTY of a SNUG PATRIMONY for the UNCERTAINTY of the continuance of my life?"

☞ If you assure one out of ten of those thus urged, you will do well, and have no reason to be discouraged; and, as to the remaining nine, you may have started in their minds new ideas on the subject, and some of them may eventually give you their applications. Therefore do not be disheartened by lack of immediate success.

HOW TO MEET OBJECTIONS.

IF an objection is not started, do not make reference to it. Never anticipate difficulties by bringing them forward yourself; but be ready at every point fairly to meet them when presented We can onlv *hint* how this may be done, in a number of cases.

1. Indebtedness.

WHEN *indebtedness* is urged as an objection, show its fallacy, e. g., thus: "If you die with debts unpaid, where will your family be?

If you assure and die, your creditors may be paid at once. Did you ever hear the assignee of a bankrupt blame him for spending money for a LIFE ASSURANCE POLICY? *Never.*"

2. WELL OFF.

IF one says he is well off, show that the rich often become poor. Mention cases that the man has known. Also urge that at his death the family would need *cash in hand.* Thus: "It might take twelve, eighteen, or twenty-four months for your executors to settle up your estate. Were you to die now, would they have enough READY CASH left them to live in the style they now live in, and meet the extra expenses incident to your decease? You think not. Then procure a generous life-policy, which would be IMMEDIATELY CONVERTIBLE INTO MONEY."

3. RELIGIOUS SCRUPLES.

SOMETIMES religious scruples exist. Show that religion does not forbid, but enjoins, prudence. Allude to the practice of *fire* insurance. Or, put the case thus: "Who is most likely to worry about the fate of his wife and children—a man with a few thousands of dollars laid up for them, or one who has made no provision for them?"

Rev. Dr. Cumming, of London, says: "The assurance of life is one of the most christian things that I know; for what is it? It is taking the load that would crush one family, and spreading it over twenty thousand families; so that a mere drop lights upon each, instead of the overwhelming torrent failing upon one. It seems to me a beautiful illustration of bearing one another's burdens. And, therefore, let every young man entering upon life, every head of a family, whether high or low, set his house in order so far as to assure his life."

4. Fears as to Safety.

WHERE doubt exists as to the safety of Assurance, show that Life companies *have* stood secure; that they cannot, if properly managed, fail; and that such companies thrive even upon the ruins of other financial concerns: for, by the mishaps of others, money is increased in value, and it is in money that these institutions deal.

Add, also, that in times of convulsions men rush into Life Assurance, thereby increasing the business of such institutions, and making it profitable. (See, also, page 24.)

5. Expensiveness.

If its expensiveness is talked of, show that it is not an expense, but an *accumulation*. It is neither more nor less than an absolutely sure investment of whatever you can, by a well-considered economy, spare, in order to procure, upon the best terms, a sufficiency to support your family, or your own old age when it has grown helpless. But at any rate how little does it cost! Ten cents a day amounts in one year to thirty-six dollars and fifty cents. This sum would secure a life-policy for a man aged twenty-three in the sum of $2,000; and if he should live to a good age the amount to be paid yearly, if anything, would be very small, or the amount and value of the policy would be largely increased. And add, "Will you not use up your income anyhow? so that what you put in here is *so much gained.*"

6. Making Money Fast.

When one urges that he is vigorous and making money, insist that from the superfluity of the present he should provide for the possible imbecility and scarcity of the future; as Joseph directed Pharaoh to lay up from the seven years of plenty against the seven years of famine.

7. Assuring One's Self.

IF one says, "I can assure myself by taking the risk as cheaply as a company can do it for me," show that his may not be an average life as to duration; that the rate of mortality is only certain with respect to a large number of persons.

8. The Savings Bank.

WHEN the objection is that it is better to deposit small moneys in the savings bank, meet it thus: Even if you *live*, it were better to put them into a Life-Policy. Suppose a person to deposit $1,000 with a Mutual Life Assurance Company on the accumulative principle (that is, to purchase a fixed policy payable at death), and $1,000 with a good and reponsible Savings Bank. Mark the result running through the twenty-five intervening years of a person's life, from 25 to 50, as shown in this Table:

If he die at the age of	HIS HEIRS WILL RECEIVE FROM The Savings Bank,	The Assurance Company,
30	$1,280	$3,425
35	1,639	3,665
40	2,097	3,886
45	2,685	4,087
50	3,437	5,273

If, then, with equal security to the depositor, Life Assurance on the Accumulative principle *pays a much larger sum to the family* than would be paid by the accumulations of a Savings Bank, ought not this mode of investment to be preferred?

9. Using Funds in Business.

DOES the objector assume that he can better use his money in his business? Put the case thus: "Suppose your profits to be twenty-five per cent., or even double that:—no matter what your prosperity. Here is a trifling periodical payment which covers an enormous risk. It covers the risk of your dying in the interim. Can your business do this, or anything approaching it? Suppose, to take the strongest case, you put $50 in your business, and at the year's end it is likely to become $250. Yet, even then you had better put your fifty dollars in an Assurance company; for, should you die before the year's end, you would thereby have secured $2,000 for your family. If you live, so much the better; thank God, and go on again, not forgetting to pay another premium in due time, lest during another year you should not be so fortunate."

10. No Family Ties.

ALTHOUGH one has no family, and may not have one, show that money may be needed in advanced age, and so explain an *endowment* or an *annuity* policy. Also, that some *relative* may be benefited by a policy; or that in this way he might like to *will* something to a benevolent or educational institution.

11. Inability to Continue.

WHERE one fears he cannot continue payments, and so may lose all that is put in, reply, "Have you not had the value of your money in the risk, as in a fire-policy?" And better, "Non-forfeiture prevents the possibility of losing what is put in:" (and so explain this beautiful arrangement.)

12. Some Other Time.

WHEN one says, "I will think of it," it is well to remind him that procrastination is not only "the thief of time," but the murderer of *opportunity:* that many a family is doomed to want from a similar delay of but a day or an hour; (refer to examples in AMERICAN MANUAL OF LIFE ASSURANCE:) that a man was lately found dead with a blank application in his pocket, which he intended to fill out "to-morrow:" that *this* is a matter of the *first* importance, and one usually attends to *important* things *first*: that he would not leave his house, store, barn, or shop uninsured a day: and, finally, that to-morrow he may not be assurable, from possible indisposition, accident, or death. Therefore,

"Shun delays; they breed remorse;
Take thy time while time is lent thee.
Creeping snails have weakest force;
Fly their fault, lest thou repent thee.
Good is best when soonest wrought,
Lingering labors come to nought."

☞ For answers to other objections (and these more fully), see AMERICAN MANUAL OF LIFE ASSURANCE.

☞ If one will not be persuaded to assure, try to find where the *sticking-point* is, and remove the difficulty by arguing the case out clearly; then, *urge to immediate action.*

CONVENIENT TABLES.

SIMPLE INTEREST TABLE,

Showing the Interest at 7 per cent., for one year, payable in advance, on any Sum from One Dollar to One Hundred Dollars.

Dol.	Int.	Dol.	Int.	Dol.	Int.	Dol.	Int.	Dol.	Int.
$1	$.07	$21	$1.38	$41	$2.69	$61	$4.00	$81	$5.31
2	.13	22	1.44	42	2.75	62	4.06	82	5.37
3	.20	23	1.51	43	2.82	63	4.13	83	5.44
4	.26	24	1.57	44	2.88	64	4.19	84	5.50
5	.33	25	1.64	45	2.95	65	4.26	85	5.57
6	.39	26	1.70	46	3.01	66	4.32	86	5.63
7	.46	27	1.77	47	3.08	67	4.39	87	5.70
8	.52	28	1.83	48	3.14	68	4.45	88	5.76
9	.29	29	1.90	49	3.21	69	4.52	89	5.83
10	.65	30	1.97	50	3.28	70	4.59	90	5.90
11	.72	31	2.03	51	3.34	71	4.65	91	5.96
12	.79	32	2.10	52	3.41	72	4.72	92	6.03
13	.85	33	2.16	53	3.47	73	4.79	93	6.09
14	.92	34	2.23	54	3.54	74	4.85	94	6.16
15	.98	35	2.29	55	3.60	75	4.91	95	6.22
16	1.05	36	2.36	56	3.67	76	4.98	96	6.29
17	1.11	37	2.42	57	3.73	77	5.04	97	6.35
18	1.18	38	2.49	58	3.80	78	5.11	98	6.42
19	1.24	39	2.55	59	3.86	79	5.17	99	6.48
20	1.31	40	2.62	60	3.93	80	5.24	100	6.56

COMPOUND INTEREST TABLES—(over.)

Table I on the following pages shows the result of Compound Interest on the Deposit of One Dollar, for any number of years not exceeding 100, at various rates. Table II shows the result of compounding an *annual payment* of One Dollar at the beginning of each year, for a term of years not exceeding 100. By the use of this Table one can ascertain what a given annual premium paid for any number of successive years will amount to at say six per cent. Multiply the annual premium by the sum opposite the number of years, under 6 per cent., in Table II; this will give the desired result. The same rule applies in relation to Endowment Premiums. To ascertain what rate of interest has been realized by the payment in full of an annual premium for a term of years, divide the total amount of Policy with additions by the annual premium. Then find, in Table II, the number corresponding nearest to the quotient, in the line opposite the number of years the premiums have been paid. The rate of interest at the head of the column containing such number will express approximately the rate realized on the investment. By the combined use of Tables I and II, Results of Five, Ten, or Fifteen Payment Policies may be calculated for any term of years.

I. COMPOUND INTEREST.

Showing the Amount of $1 improved at Compound Interest, for any number of **years** not exceeding 100.

Years.	4 per Ct.	4½ per Ct.	5 per Ct.	6 per Ct.	7 per Ct.	8 per Ct.
1	1.040000	1.045000	1.050000	1.060000	1.070000	1.080000
2	1.081600	1.092025	1.102500	1.123600	1.144900	1.166400
3	1.124864	1.141166	1.157625	1.191016	1.225043	1.259712
4	1.169859	1.192519	1.215506	1.262477	1.310796	1.360489
5	1.216653	1.246182	1.276282	1.338226	1.402552	1.469328
6	1.265319	1.302260	1.340096	1.418519	1.500730	1.586874
7	1.315932	2.360862	1.407100	1.503630	1.605781	1.713824
8	1.368569	1.422101	1.477455	1.593848	1.718186	1.850930
9	1.423312	1.486095	1.551328	1.689479	1.838459	1.999005
10	1.480244	1.552969	1.628895	1.790843	1.967151	2.158925
11	1.539454	1.622853	1.710339	1.898299	2.104852	2.331639
12	1.601032	1.695881	1.795856	2.012196	2.252192	2.518170
13	1.665074	1.772196	1.885649	2.132928	2.409845	2.719624
14	1.731676	1.851945	1.979932	2.260904	2.578534	2.937194
15	1.800944	1.935282	2.078928	2.396558	2.759032	3.172169
16	1.872981	2.022370	2.182875	2.540352	2.952164	3.425943
17	1.947901	2.113377	2.292018	2.692773	3.158815	3.700018
18	2.025817	2.208479	2.406619	2.854339	3.379932	3.996020
19	2.106849	2.307860	2.526950	3.025600	3.616528	4.315701
20	2.191123	2.411714	2.653298	3.207135	3.869684	4.660957
21	2.278768	2.520241	2.785963	3.399564	4.140562	5.033834
22	2.369919	2.633652	2.925261	3.603537	4.430402	5.436540
23	2.464716	2.752166	3.071524	3.819750	4.740530	5.871464
24	2.563303	2.876014	3.225100	4.048935	5.072367	6.341181
25	2.665836	3.005434	3.386355	4.291871	5.427433	6.848475
26	2.772470	3.140679	3.555673	4.549483	5.807353	7.396353
27	2.883369	3.282010	3.733456	4.822346	6.213868	7.988061
28	2.998703	3.429700	3.920129	5.111687	6.648838	8.627106
29	3.118651	3.584036	4.116136	5.418388	7.114257	9.317275
30	3.243398	3.745318	4.321942	5.743491	7.612255	10.062657
31	3.373133	3.913857	4.538039	6.088101	8.145113	10.867669
32	3.508059	4.089981	4.764941	6.453387	8.715271	11.737083
33	3.648381	4.274030	5.003189	6.840590	9.325340	12.676050
34	3.794316	4.466362	5.253348	7.251025	9.978114	13.690134
35	3.946089	4.667348	5.516015	7.686087	10.676581	14.785344
36	4.103933	4.877378	5.791816	8.147252	11.423942	15.968172
37	4.268090	5.096860	6.081407	8.636087	12.223618	17.245626
38	4.438813	5.326219	6.385477	9.154252	13.079271	18.625276
39	4.616366	5.565899	6.704751	9.703507	13.994820	20.115298
40	4.801021	5.816365	7.039989	10.285718	14.974458	21.724522
41	4.993061	6.078101	7.391988	10.902861	16.022670	23.462483
42	5.192784	6.351615	7.761588	11.557033	17.144257	25.339482
43	5.400495	6.637438	8.149667	12.250455	18.344355	27.366640
44	5.616515	6.936123	8.557150	12.985482	19.628460	29.555972
45	5.841176	7.248248	8.985008	13.764611	21.002452	31.920449
46	6.074823	7.574420	9.434258	14.590487	22.472623	34.474085
47	6.317816	7.915268	9.905971	15.465917	24.045707	37.232012
48	6.570528	8.271456	10.401270	16.393872	25.728907	40.210573
49	6.833349	8.643671	10.921333	17.377504	27.529930	43.427419
50	7.106683	9.032636	11.467400	18.420154	29.457025	46.901613

COMPOUND INTEREST, I.—(Continued.)

Showing the Amount of $1 improved at Compound Interest, for any number of years not exceeding 100.

Years.	4 per Ct.	4½ per Ct.	5 per Ct.	6 per Ct.	7 per Ct.	8 per Ct.
51	7.390951	9.439105	12.040770	19.525364	31.519017	50.653742
52	7.686589	9.863865	12.642808	20.696885	33.725348	54.706041
53	7.994052	10.307739	13.274949	21.938698	36.086122	59.082524
54	8.313814	10.771587	13.938696	23.255020	38.612151	63.809126
55	8.646367	11.256308	14.635631	24.650322	41.315001	68.913856
56	8.992222	11.762842	15.367412	26.129341	44.207052	74.426965
57	9.351910	12.292170	16.135783	27.697101	47.301545	80.381122
58	9.725987	12.845318	16.942572	29.358927	50.612653	86.811612
59	10.115026	13.423357	17.789701	31.120463	54.155539	93.756540
60	10.519627	14.027408	18.679186	32.987691	57.946427	101.257064
61	10.940413	14.658641	19.613145	34.966952	62.002677	109.357629
62	11.378029	15.318280	20.593802	37.064969	66.342864	118.106239
63	11.833150	16.007603	21.623493	39.288868	70-986865	127.554738
64	12.306476	16.727945	22.704667	41-646200	75.955945	137.759117
65	12.798735	17.480702	23-839901	44.144972	81.272861	148.779847
66	13.310685	18.267334	25.031896	46.793670	86.961962	160.682234
67	13.843112	19.089364	26.283490	49.601290	93.049299	173.536813
68	14.396836	19.948385	27.597665	52.577368	99.562750	187.419758
69	14.972710	20.846063	28.977548	55.732010	106.532142	202.413339
70	15.571618	21.784136	30.426426	59-075930	113.989392	218.606406
71	16.194483	22.764422	31.947747	62.620486	121.968650	236.094918
72	16.842262	23.788821	33.545134	66.377415	130.506455	254.982512
73	17.515953	24.859318	45.222391	70.360378	139.641907	275.381113
74	18.216591	25.977987	36.983510	74.582001	149.416840	297.411602
75	18.945255	27.146996	38.832686	79.056921	159.876019	321.204530
76	19.703065	28.368611	40.774320	83.800336	171.067341	346.900892
77	20.491187	29.645199	42.813036	88.828356	183.042054	374.652964
78	21.310835	30.979233	44.953688	94.158058	195.854998	404.625201
79	22.163268	32.373298	47.201372	99.807541	209.564848	436.995217
80	23.049799	33.830096	49.561441	105.795993	224.234388	471.954834
81	23.971791	35.352451	52.039513	112.143753	239.930795	509.711221
82	24.930663	36.943311	54.641489	118.872378	256.725950	550.488119
83	25.927889	38.605760	57.373563	126.004721	274.696767	594.527168
84	26.965005	40.343019	60.242241	133.565004	293.925541	642.089342
85	28.043605	42.158455	63.254353	141.578904	314.500328	693.456489
86	29.165349	44.055586	96.417071	150.073639	336.515351	748.933008
87	30.331963	46.038087	69.737925	159.078057	360.071426	808.847649
88	31.545242	48.109801	73.224821	168.622740	385.276426	873.555461
89	32.807051	50.274742	76.886062	178.740105	412.245776	943.439897
90	34.119333	52.537105	80.730365	189.464511	441.102980	1018.91509
91	35.484107	54.901275	84.766883	200.832382	471.980188	1100.42830
92	36.903471	57.371832	89.005227	212.882325	505.018802	1188.46256
93	38.379610	59.953565	93.455489	225.655264	540.370118	1283.53956
94	39.914794	62.651475	98.128263	239.194580	578.196026	1386.22273
95	41.511386	65.470792	103.034676	253.546255	618.669748	1497.12055
96	43.171841	68.416977	108.186410	268.759030	661.976630	1616.89019
97	44.898715	71.495741	113.595731	284.884572	708.314994	1746.24141
98	46.694664	74.7-3050	119.275517	301.977646	757.897044	1885.94072
99	48.562450	78.075137	125.239293	320.096305	810.949837	2036.81598
100	50.504948	81.588518	131.501258	339.302084	867.716326	2199.76126

COMPOUND INTEREST, II.

The amount of $1 per annum in any number of Years.

Years.	4 per Cent.	4½ per Cent.	5 per Cent.	6 per Cent.
1	1.000000	1.000000	1.000000	1.000000
2	2.040000	2.045000	2.050000	2.060000
3	3.121600	3.137025	3.152500	3.183600
4	4.246464	4.278191	4.310125	4.374616
5	5.416323	5.470710	5.525631	5.637093
6	6.632975	6.716892	6.801913	6.975319
7	7.898294	8.019152	8.142008	8.393838
8	9.214226	9.380014	9.549109	9.897468
9	10.582795	10.802114	11.026564	11.491316
10	12.006107	12.288209	12.577893	13.180795
11	13.486351	13.841179	14.206787	14.971643
12	15.025805	15.464032	15.917127	16.869941
13	16.626838	17.159913	17.712983	18.882138
14	18.291911	18.932109	19.598632	21.015066
15	20.023588	20.784054	21.578564	23.275970
16	21.824531	22.719337	23.657492	25.672528
17	23.697512	24.741707	25.840366	28.212880
18	25.645413	26.855084	28.132385	30.905653
19	27.671229	29.063562	30.539004	33.759992
20	29.778079	31.371423	33.065954	36.785591
21	31.969202	33.783137	35.719252	39.992727
22	34.247970	36.303378	38.505214	43.392290
23	36.617889	38.937030	41.430475	46.995828
24	39.082604	41.689196	44.501999	50.815577
25	41.645908	44.565210	47.727099	54.864512
26	44.311745	47.570645	51.113454	59.156383
27	47.084214	50.711324	54.669126	63.705766
28	49.967583	53.993333	58.402583	68.528112
29	52.966286	57.423033	62.322712	73.639798
30	56.084938	61.007070	66.438848	79.058186
31	59.328335	64.752388	70.760790	84.801677
32	62.701469	68.666245	75.298829	90.889778
33	66.209527	72.756226	80.063771	97.343165
34	69.857909	77.030256	85.066959	104.184755
35	73.652225	81.496618	90.320307	111.434780
36	77.598314	86.163966	95.836323	119.120867
37	81.702246	91.041344	101.628139	127.268119
38	85.970336	96.138205	107.709546	135.904206
39	90.409150	101.464424	114.095023	145.058458
40	95.025516	107.030323	120.799774	154.761966
41	99.826536	112.846688	127.839763	165.047684
42	104.819598	118.924789	135.231751	175.950545
43	110.012382	125.276404	142.993339	187.507577
44	115.412877	131.913842	151.143006	199.758032
45	121.029392	138.849965	159.700156	212.743514
46	126.870568	146.098214	168.685164	226.508125
47	132.945390	153.672633	178.119422	241.098612
48	139.263206	161.587902	188.025393	256.564529
49	145.833734	169.859357	199.426663	272.958401
50	152.667084	178.503028	209.347996	290.335905

COMPOUND INTEREST, II.—(Continued.)

The amount of $1 per annum in any number of Years.

Years.	4 per Cent.	4½ per Cent.	5 per Cent.	6 per Cent.
51	159.773767	187.535665	220.815395	308.756059
52	167.164718	196.974769	232.856165	328.281422
53	174.851306	206.838634	245.498974	348.978308
54	182.845359	217.146373	258.773922	370.917006
55	191.159173	227.917959	272.712618	394.172027
56	199.805540	239.174268	287.348249	418.822348
57	208.797762	250.937110	302.715662	444.951689
58	218.149672	263.229280	318.851445	472.648790
59	227.875659	276.074597	335.794017	502.007718
60	237.990685	289.497954	353.583718	533.128181
61	248.510313	303.525362	372.262904	566.115872
62	259.450725	318.184003	391.876049	601.082824
63	270.828754	333.502283	412.469851	638.147793
64	282.661904	349.509886	434.093344	677.436661
65	294.968381	366.237831	456.798011	719.082861
66	307.767116	383.718533	480.637912	763.227832
67	321.074800	401.985867	505.669807	810.021502
68	334.920912	421.075231	531.953298	859.622792
69	349.317749	441.023617	559.550963	912.200160
70	364.290459	461.869680	588.528511	967.932170
71	379.862077	483.653815	618.954936	1027.008100
72	396.956560	506.418237	650.902683	1089.628586
73	412.898823	530.207057	684.447817	1156.006301
74	430.414776	555.066375	719.670208	1226.366679
75	448.631367	581.044362	756.653718	1300.948680
76	467.576621	608.191358	795.486404	1380.005601
77	487.279686	636.559969	836.260725	1463.805937
78	507.770874	666.205168	879.073761	1552.634293
79	529.081708	697.184401	924.027449	1646.792350
80	551.244977	729.557699	971.228821	1746.599891
81	574.294776	763.387795	1020.790262	1852.395885
82	598.266567	798.740246	1072.829775	1964.539638
83	623.197230	835.683557	1127.471264	2083.412016
84	649.125119	874.289317	1184.844827	2209.416737
85	676.090124	914.632336	1245.087069	2342.981741
86	704.133728	956.790791	1308.341422	2484.560646
87	733.299078	1000 846377	1374.758493	2634.634285
88	763.631041	1046.884464	1444.496418	2793.712342
89	795.176282	1094.994265	1517.721239	2962.335082
90	827.983334	1145.269007	1594.607301	3141.075187
91	862.102667	1197.806112	1675.337666	3330.539698
92	897.586774	1252.707387	1760.104549	3531.372080
93	934.490245	1310.079219	1849.109777	3744.254405
94	972.869854	1370.032784	1942.565265	3969.909669
95	1012.784649	1432.684259	2040.693529	4209.104250
96	1054.296035	1498.155051	2143.728205	4462.650505
97	1097.467876	1566.572028	2251.914615	4731.409535
98	1142.366591	1638.067770	2365.510346	5016.294107
99	1189.061255	1712.780819	2484.785864	5318.271753
100	1237.623705	1790.855956	2610.025157	5638.368059

COMPOUND INTEREST, II.—(CONTINUED.)

The amount of $1 per annum in any number of years.

Years.	7 per Cent.	8 per Cent.	9 per Cent.	10 per Cent.
1	1.000000	1.000000	1.000000	1.000000
2	2.070000	2.080000	2.090000	2.100000
3	3.214900	3.246400	3.278100	3.310000
4	4.439943	4.506112	4.573129	4.641000
5	5.750739	5.866601	5.984711	6.105100
6	7.153291	7.335929	7.523335	7.715610
7	8.654021	8.922803	9.200435	9.487171
8	10.259803	10.636628	11.028474	11.435888
9	11.977989	12.487558	13.021036	13.579477
10	13.816448	14.486562	15.192930	15.937425
11	15.783599	16.645487	17.560293	18.531167
12	17.888451	18.977126	20.140720	21.384284
13	20.140643	21.495297	22.953385	24.522712
14	22.550488	24.214920	26.019189	27.974983
15	25.129022	27.152114	29.360916	31.772482
16	27.888054	30.324283	33.003399	35.949730
17	30.840217	33.750226	36.973705	40.544703
18	33.999033	37.450244	41.301338	45.599173
19	37.378965	41.446263	46.018458	51.159090
20	40.995492	45.761964	51.160120	57.274999
21	44.865177	50.422921	56.764530	64.002499
22	49.005739	55.456755	62.873338	71.402749
23	53.436141	60.893296	69.531939	79.543024
24	58.176671	66.764759	76.789813	88.497327
25	63.249038	73.105940	84.700896	98.347059
26	68.676470	79.954415	93.323977	109.181765
27	74.483823	87.350768	102.723135	121.099942
28	80.697691	95.338830	112.968217	134.209936
29	87.346529	103.965936	124.135356	148.630930
30	94.460786	113.283211	136.307539	164.494023
31	102.073041	123.345868	149.575217	181.943425
32	110.218154	134.213537	164.036987	201.137767
33	118.933425	145.950620	179.800315	222.251544
34	128.258765	158.626670	196.982344	245.476699
35	138.236878	172.316804	215.710755	271.024368
36	148.913460	187.102148	236.124723	299.126805
37	160.337402	203.070320	258.375948	330.039486
38	172.561020	220.315945	282.629783	364.043434
39	185.640292	238.941221	309.066463	401.447778
40	199.635112	259.056519	337.882445	442.292556
41	214.609570	280.781040	369.291865	487.851811
42	230.632240	304.243523	403.528133	537.636992
43	247.776496	329.583005	440.845665	592.400692
44	266.120851	356.949646	481.521775	652.640761
45	285.749311	386.505617	525.858734	718.904837
46	306.751763	418.426067	574.186021	791.795321
47	329.224386	452.900152	626.862762	871.974853
48	353.270093	490.132164	684.280411	960.172338
49	378.999000	530.342737	746.865648	1057.189572
50	406.528929	573.770156	815.083556	1163.908529

COMPOUND INTEREST, II.—(CONTINUED.)

The amount of $1 per annum in any number of years.

Years.	7 per Cent.	8 per Cent.	9 per Cent.	10 per Cent.
51	435.985955	620.671769	889.44.070	1281.299382
52	467.504971	671.325510	970.490773	1410.429320
53	501.230319	726.031551	1058.834943	1552.472252
54	537.316442	785.114075	1155.130088	1708.719477
55	575.928593	848.923201	1260.091796	1880.591425
56	617.243594	917.837058	1374.500057	2069.650567
57	661.450646	992.264022	1499.205063	2277.615624
58	708.752191	1072.645144	1635.133518	2506.377186
59	759.364844	1159.456755	1783.295535	2758.014905
60	813.520383	1253.213296	1944.792133	3034.816395
61	871.466810	1354.470360	2120.823425	3339.298035
62	933.469487	1463.827988	2312.697533	3674.227838
63	999.812351	1581.934227	2521.840311	4042.650622
64	1070.799216	1709.488966	2749.805939	4447.915685
65	1146.755161	1847.248083	2998.288474	4893.707253
66	122S.028022	1996.027929	3269.134436	5384.077978
67	1314.989983	2156.710164	3564.356535	5923.485776
68	1408.039282	2330.246977	3886.148624	6516.834354
69	1507.602032	2517.666735	4236.902000	7169.517789
70	1614.134174	2720.080074	4619.223180	7887.469568
71	1728.123566	2938.686480	5035.953266	8677.216525
72	1850.092216	3174.781398	5490.189060	9545.938177
73	1980.598671	3429.763910	5985.306075	10501.531995
74	2120.240578	3705.145023	6524.983622	11552.685195
75	2269.657419	4002.556624	7113.232148	12708.953714
76	2429.533438	4323.761154	7754.423041	13980.849085
77	2600.600779	4670.662047	8453.321115	15379.933994
78	2783.642833	5045.315011	9215.120015	16918.927393
79	2979.497831	5449.940211	10045.480817	18611.820133
80	3189.062680	5886.935428	10950.574090	20474.002146
81	3413.297067	6358.890263	11937.125758	22522.402360
82	3653.227862	6868.601484	13012.467077	24775.642596
83	3909.953812	7419.089602	14184.589114	27254.206856
84	4184.650579	8013.616770	15462.202134	29980.627542
85	4478.576120	8655.706112	16854.800326	32979.690296
86	4793.076448	9349.162601	18372.732355	36278.659326
87	5129.591799	10098.095609	20027.278267	39907.525258
88	5489.663225	10906.943258	21830.733311	43899.277784
89	5874.939651	11780.498718	23796.499309	48290.205562
90	6287.185427	12723.938616	25939.184247	53120.226119
91	6728.288407	13742.853705	28274.710829	58433.248730
92	7200.268595	14843.282002	30826.434804	64277.573603
93	7705.287397	16031.744562	33595.273936	70706.330964
94	8245.657515	17315.284127	36619.848590	77777.964060
95	8823.853541	18701.506857	39916.634964	85556.760466
96	9442.523288	20198.627405	43510.132110	94113.436513
97	10104.499919	21815.517598	47427.044000	103525.780164
98	10812.814913	23561.759006	51696.477960	113879.358180
90	11570.711957	25447.699726	56350.160977	125268.293998
100	12381.661794	27484.515704	61422.675465	137796.123398

STANDARD MORTALITY TABLES.

DESCRIPTION.*

No. 1.—Halley's Breslau Table.

This Table was deduced by the celebrated Astronomer Edmund Halley, from a series of life registers kept by Dr. Neumann in the city of Breslau in Silesia during the years 1687–91, and was the first Life Table which had any pretensions to accuracy. It was, however, regarded as inapplicable to English lives, and has, consequently, never been used by English companies. By arranging the numbers in the second column of this Table, Dr. Halley, all unconsciously, laid the foundation of the science of life contingencies.

No. 2.—Price's London Table.

This Table was arranged by Dr. Richard Price from the bills of mortality recorded in London during the years 1759–1768. It gives a high rate of mortality, and has not been used in the business of Life Assurance.

No. 3.—Price's Swedish Table.

This was the first National Life Table ever made, and was composed by the eminent Statistician Dr. Richard Price, from data obtained by M. Wargentin, of Stockholm, from seven different enumerations of the whole population of the Kingdom of Sweden, each repeated at the

* For the purpose of securing absolute accuracy, the tables which follow (with the descriptive matter) are those carefully collated and published in the Insurance Reports of the State of New York.

end of three years, viz., in 1757, 1760, 1763, 1766, 1769, 1772, and 1775. It is commended for its general accuracy, but, owing apparently to national preferences, has not been used in England.

No. 4.—Deparcieux's French Table.

This Table was calculated by M. Deparcieux from the lists kept of the nominees of the Tontines of Paris and from the records of the deaths of Parisian annuitants from 1696 to 1742. It has been well approved as giving a near approximation to the expectation of assured lives.

The results of M. Deparcieux's calculations were afterward verified by comparison with the mortuary registers of several religious houses of both sexes in France.

This Table is referred to by Francis Baily in his Treatise upon the Doctrine of Annuities and Assurances (p. 14), published in 1813, as particularly fitted to form a proper basis for determining the value of annuities.

No. 5.—Price's Northampton Table.

This Table was formed by Dr. Richard Price from registers kept in the Parish of All-Saints in the town of Northampton, England, during the years 1735 to 1780. Although exceedingly unjust in giving a too high rate of mortality, particularly for the younger and middle ages, it was the first Life Table brought into use as a basis for the computation of Life premiums, having been adopted by the Equitable on its establishment in the year 1762. The Northampton Table long continued in much favor with the companies, as insuring an abundantly safe rate of premium; so much so, indeed, as to secure a higer profit, without loading, than is obtained under many other Tables even with the addition of a loading of 20 or 30 per cent. This Table is still used by a majority of the old Life Offices in England as the basis for their rates of premium. In making valuations, however, the results are generally checked by calculations on the Carlisle or some other modern Table.

No. 6.—Milne's Carlisle Table.

This Table was formed by the eminent Actuary Joshua Milne, from the observations of Dr. Heysham on the mortality of Carlisle, England, for the years 1778–87. Though somewhat defective in graduation, it is far more satisfactory than the Northampton Table in its approach to accuracy; for which reason it is extensively used in England and very generally in this country.

No. 7.—Davies's Equitable Table.

Constructed by the distinguished Actuary Griffith Davies, of London, and revised by Mr. Morgan in 1834. This was the first Table based upon the records of assured lives, being the experience of the Equitable Society from its foundation in 1762 to 1829.

No. 8.—Actuaries' or Combined Experience Table.

This Table is based upon the recorded experience of seventeen Life Companies in England, and was deduced from 62,537 assurances, under the superintendence of a committee of accomplished actuaries. The Table was published by Actuary Jenkin Jones in 1843, and furnishes a very accurate graduation of assured lives.

No. 9.—QUETELET'S BELGIAN TABLE.

This Table was compiled and published in 1856 by the distinguished philosopher ADOLPHE QUETELET, of Brussels. It shows a higher rate of mortality than the English Tables. In the form here presented, the Table gives the combined decrement and expectation of male and female lives.

No. 10.—FARR'S ENGLISH TABLE No. 1.

For this very accurate Table the public are indebted to the philanthrophic and praiseworthy efforts of the indefatigable physician WILLIAM FARR, of London. It was compiled from the entire census returns of lives and deaths at all ages, in the realm of England, during the year 1841, and published in the Sixth Report of the Registrar-General.

No. 11—FARR'S ENGLISH TABLE No. 2.

This was calculated by Dr. WILLIAM FARR, subsequently to his Table No. 1, from the deaths throughout the whole of England dusing the seven years 1838–44. From these data the calculations were made according to a plan recommended by Professor DE MORGAN and Mr. GRIFFITH DAVIES.

No. 12.—FARR'S ENGLISH TABLE No. 3.

The rate of mortality deduced from this Table is higher than is given by the Carlisle Table or by either of the two former English Life Tables of the author. It is more regular in its graduation than the Carlisle Table, while at the same time its rate approximates more nearly that assigned to American life.

I. BRESLAU TABLE (Edmund Halley).

Age.	Living.	Dying.	Expectation.	Age.	Living.	Dying.	Expectation.
1	1000	145	33.22	46	387	10	19.05
2	855	57	37.77	47	377	10	18.55
3	798	38	39.43	48	367	10	18.04
4	760	28	40.38	49	357	11	17.53
5	732	22	40.90	50	346	11	17.07
6	710	18	41.16	51	335	11	16.61
7	692	12	41.22	52	324	11	16.16
8	680	10	40.94	53	313	11	15.71
9	670	9	40.54	54	302	10	15.26
10	661	8	40.08	55	292	10	14.77
11	653	7	39.57	56	282	10	14.27
12	646	6	38.99	57	272	10	13.79
13	640	6	38.35	58	262	10	12.91
14	634	6	37.71	59	252	10	12.79
15	628	6	37.07	60	242	10	12.30
16	622	6	36.42	61	232	10	11.77
17	616	6	35.77	62	222	10	11.32
18	610	6	35.12	63	212	10	10.83
19	604	6	34.46	64	202	10	10.24
20	598	6	33.80	65	192	10	9.86
21	592	6	33.14	66	182	10	9.37
22	586	7	32.49	67	172	10	8.89
23	579	6	31.85	68	162	10	8.40
24	573	6	31.29	69	152	10	7.93
25	567	7	30.51	70	142	11	7.45
26	560	7	29.87	71	131	11	7.03
27	553	7	29.26	72	120	11	6.64
28	546	7	28.63	73	109	11	6.25
29	539	8	27.99	74	98	10	5.89
30	531	8	27.41	75	88	10	5.51
31	523	8	26.82	76	78	10	5.15
32	515	8	26.23	77	68	10	4.84
33	507	8	25.64	78	58	9	4.59
34	499	9	25.04	79	49	8	4.34
35	490	9	24.50	80	41	7	4.08
36	481	9	24.15	81	34	6	3.80
37	472	9	23.60	82	28	5	3.54
38	463	9	23.26	83	23	4	3.19
39	454	9	22.72	84	19	4	2.76
40	445	9	22.16	85	15	4	2.37
41	436	9	21.61	86	11	3	2.05
42	427	10	21.06	87	8	3	1.63
43	417	10	20.55	88	5	2	0.80
44	407	10	20.04	89	3	2	0.33
45	397	10	19.53	90	1	1	0.00

II. LONDON TABLE (Richard Price).

Age.	Living.	Dying.	Expectation.	Age.	Living.	Dying.	Expectation.
0	1518	486	17.90	46	262	10	
1	1032	200		47	252	10	
2	832	85		48	242	9	
3	747	59		49	233	9	
4	688	42		50	224	9	15.84
5	646	23	35.28	51	215	9	
6	623	20		52	206	8	
7	603	14		53	198	8	
8	589	12		54	190	7	
9	577	10		55	183	7	13.91
10	567	9	34.91	56	176	7	
11	558	9		57	169	7	
12	549	8		58	162	7	
13	541	7		59	155	8	
14	534	6		60	147	8	11.69
15	528	6	33.32	61	139	7	
16	522	7		62	132	7	
17	515	7		63	125	7	
18	508	7		64	118	7	
19	501	7		65	111	7	9.69
20	494	7	29.37	66	104	7	
21	487	8		67	97	7	
22	479	8		68	90	7	
23	471	8		69	83	7	
24	463	8		70	76	6	8.00
25	455	8	26.66	71	70	6	
26	447	8		72	64	6	
27	439	8		73	58	5	
28	431	9		74	53	5	
29	422	9		75	48	5	6.27
30	413	9	24.11	76	43	5	
31	404	9		77	38	5	
32	395	9		78	33	4	
33	386	9		79	29	4	
34	377	9		80	25	3	4.86
35	368	9	21.76	81	22	3	
36	359	9		82	19	3	
37	350	9		83	16	3	
38	341	9		84	13	2	
39	332	10		85	11	2	3.04
40	322	10	19.50	86	9	2	
41	312	10		87	7	2	
42	302	10		88	5	1	
43	292	10		89	4	1	
44	282	10		90	3	1	
45	272	10	17.63				

III. SWEDISH TABLE (Richard Price).

Age.	Living.	Dying.	Expectation.	Age.	Living.	Dying.	Expectation.
0	10000	2195	34.42	49	3924	78	19.09
1	7805	509	42.95	50	3846	85	18.46
2	7296	344	44.92	51	3761	87	17.87
3	6952	245	46.11	52	3674	90	17.29
4	6707	143	46.78	53	3584	90	16.70
5	6564	122	46.79	54	3494	91	16.12
6	6442	105	46.66	55	3403	91	15.53
7	6337	87	46.43	56	3312	92	14.95
8	6250	73	46.07	57	3220	95	14.37
9	6177	62	45.61	58	3125	95	13.79
10	6115	54	45.07	59	3030	100	13.21
11	6061	45	44.38	60	2930	108	12.63
12	6016	42	43.70	61	2822	114	12.12
13	5974	38	43.01	62	2708	118	11.62
14	5936	37	42.33	63	2590	118	11.11
15	5899	37	41.64	64	2472	118	10.61
16	5862	40	40.92	65	2354	118	10.10
17	5822	40	40.19	66	2236	118	9.62
18	5782	42	39.47	67	2118	121	9.15
19	5740	43	38.74	68	1997	124	8.67
20	5697	47	38.02	69	1873	124	8.20
21	5650	47	37.33	70	1749	127	7.72
22	5603	48	36.64	71	1622	133	7.32
23	5555	48	35.96	72	1489	135	6.89
24	5507	50	35.27	73	1354	140	6.53
25	5457	50	34.58	74	1214	130	6.23
26	5407	52	33.91	75	1084	121	5.91
27	5355	54	33.23	76	963	115	5.59
28	5301	55	32.56	77	848	105	5.28
29	5246	55	31.88	78	743	95	4.96
30	5191	59	31.21	79	648	90	4.61
31	5132	60	30.57	80	558	90	4.28
32	5072	62	29.94	81	468	84	4.01
33	5010	63	29.30	82	384	75	3.80
34	4947	63	28.67	83	309	65	3.57
35	4884	59	28.03	84	244	55	3.39
36	4825	58	27.31	85	189	45	3.23
37	4767	58	26.68	86	144	35	3.09
38	4709	58	26.01	87	109	27	2.92
39	4651	60	25.33	88	82	20	2.71
40	4591	65	24.66	89	62	15	2.43
41	4526	73	24.05	90	47	14	2.05
42	4453	78	23.44	91	33	12	1.71
43	4375	78	22.83	92	21	10	1.40
44	4297	78	22.22	93	11	6	1.23
45	4219	76	21.61	94	5	3	1.10
46	4143	74	20.98	95	2	1	1.00
47	4069	72	20.35	96	1	1	0.00
48	3997	73	19.72	97	0		

IV. FRENCH TABLE (M. Deparcieux).

Age.	Living.	Dying.	Expectation.	Age.	Living.	Dying.	Expectation.
3	1000	30	47.71	49	590	9	21.07
4	970	22	48.17	50	581	10	20.38
5	948	18	48.27	51	571	11	19.73
6	930	15	48.20	52	560	11	19.11
7	915	13	47.98	53	549	11	18.48
8	902	12	47.66	54	538	12	17.85
9	890	10	47.30	55	526	12	17.25
10	880	8	46.83	56	514	12	16.64
11	872	6	46.26	57	502	13	16.02
12	866	6	45.58	58	489	13	15.44
13	860	6	44.89	59	476	13	14.84
14	854	6	44.20	60	463	13	14.25
15	848	6	43.51	61	450	13	13.65
16	842	7	42.82	62	437	14	13.04
17	835	7	42.17	63	423	14	12.43
18	828	7	41.52	64	409	14	11.86
19	821	7	40.87	65	395	15	11.26
20	814	8	40.22	66	380	16	10.69
21	806	8	39.62	67	364	17	10.14
22	798	8	39.00	68	347	18	9.61
23	790	8	38.40	69	329	19	9.11
24	782	8	37.78	70	310	19	8.64
25	774	8	37.17	71	291	20	8.17
26	766	8	36.55	72	271	20	7.73
27	758	8	35.93	73	251	20	7.31
28	750	8	35.30	74	231	20	6.90
29	742	8	34.69	75	211	19	6.50
30	734	8	34.06	76	192	19	6.10
31	726	8	33.29	77	173	19	5.71
32	718	8	32.80	78	154	18	5.36
33	710	8	32.16	79	136	18	5.00
34	702	8	31.52	80	118	17	4.69
35	694	8	30.88	81	101	16	4.39
36	686	8	30.23	82	85	14	4.01
37	678	7	29.58	83	71	12	3.84
38	671	7	28.89	84	59	11	3.52
39	664	7	28.18	85	48	10	3.21
40	657	7	27.48	86	38	9	2.92
41	650	7	26.77	87	29	7	2.67
42	643	7	26.06	88	22	6	2.36
43	636	7	25.34	89	16	5	2.06
44	629	7	24.62	90	11	4	1.77
45	622	7	23.89	91	7	3	1.50
46	615	8	23.15	92	4	2	1.25
47	607	8	22.45	93	2	1	1.00
48	599	9	21.74	94	1	1	0.00

·V. NORTHAMPTON TABLE (Richard Price).

Age.	Living.	Dying.	Expectation.	Age.	Living.	Dying.	Expectation.
0	11650	3000	25.18	49	2936	79	18.49
1	8650	1367	32.74	50	2857	81	17.99
2	7283	502	37.79	51	2776	82	17.50
3	6781	335	39.55	52	2694	82	17.02
4	6446	197	40.58	53	2612	82	16.54
5	6249	184	40.84	54	2530	82	16.06
6	6065	140	41.07	55	2448	82	15.58
7	5925	110	41.03	56	2366	82	15.10
8	5815	80	40.79	57	2284	82	14.63
9	5735	60	40.36	58	2202	82	14.15
10	5675	52	39.78	59	2120	82	13.68
11	5623	50	39.14	60	2038	82	13.21
12	5573	50	38.49	61	1956	82	12.75
13	5523	50	37.83	62	1874	81	12.28
14	5473	50	37.17	63	1793	81	11.81
15	5423	50	36.51	64	1712	80	11.35
16	5373	53	35.85	65	1632	80	10.88
17	5320	58	35.20	66	1552	80	10.42
18	5262	63	34.58	67	1472	80	9.96
19	5199	67	33.99	68	1392	80	9.59
20	5132	72	33.43	69	1312	80	9.05
21	5060	75	32.90	70	1232	80	8.60
22	4985	75	32.39	71	1152	80	8.17
23	4910	75	31.88	72	1072	80	7.74
24	4835	75	31.36	73	992	80	7.33
25	4760	75	30.85	74	912	80	6.92
26	4685	75	30.33	75	832	80	6.54
27	4610	75	29.82	76	752	77	6.18
28	4535	75	29.30	77	675	73	5.83
29	4460	75	28.79	78	602	68	5.48
30	4385	75	28.27	79	534	65	5.11
31	4310	75	27.76	80	469	63	4.75
32	4235	75	27.24	81	406	60	4.41
33	4160	75	26.72	82	346	57	4.09
34	4085	75	26.20	83	289	55	3.80
35	4010	75	25.68	84	234	48	3.58
36	3935	75	25.16	85	186	41	3.37
37	3860	75	24.64	86	145	34	3.19
38	3785	75	24.12	87	111	28	3.01
39	3710	75	23.60	88	83	21	2.86
40	3635	76	23.08	89	62	16	2.66
41	3569	77	22.56	90	46	12	2.41
42	3482	78	22.04	91	34	10	2.09
43	3404	78	21.54	92	24	8	1.75
44	3326	78	21.03	93	16	7	1.37
45	3248	78	20.52	94	9	5	1.05
46	3170	78	20.02	95	4	3	0.75
47	3092	78	19.51	96	1	1	0.50
48	3014	78	19.00				

VI. CARLISLE TABLE (Joshua Milne).

Age.	Living.	Dying.	Expectation.	Age.	Living.	Dying.	Expectation.
0	10000	1539	38.721	53	4211	68	18.972
1	8461	682	44.674	54	4143	70	18.275
2	7779	505	47.546	55	4073	73	17.580
3	7274	276	49.812	56	4000	76	16.892
4	6998	201	50.757	57	3924	82	16.209
5	6797	121	51.244	58	3842	93	15.545
6	6676	82	51.163	59	3749	106	14.918
7	6594	58	50.793	60	3643	122	14.337
8	6536	43	50.240	61	3521	126	13.817
9	6493	33	49.569	62	3395	127	13.311
10	6460	29	48.820	63	3268	125	12.809
11	6431	31	48.038	64	3143	125	12.299
12	6400	32	47.268	65	3018	124	11.787
13	6368	33	46.503	66	2894	123	11.271
14	6335	35	45.742	67	2771	123	10.749
15	6300	39	44.994	68	2648	123	10.225
16	6261	42	44.271	69	2525	124	9 699
17	6219	43	43.567	70	2401	124	9.147
18	6176	43	42.866	71	2277	134	8.646
19	6133	43	42.163	72	2143	146	8.156
20	6090	43	41.458	73	1977	156	7.715
21	6047	42	40.749	74	1841	166	7.327
22	6005	42	40.030	75	1675	160	7.003
23	5963	42	39.309	76	1515	156	6.690
24	5921	42	38.584	77	1359	146	6.401
25	5879	43	37.856	78	1213	132	6.111
26	5836	43	37.131	79	1081	128	5.796
27	5793	45	36.403	80	953	116	5.507
28	5748	50	35.684	81	837	112	5.201
29	5698	56	34.993	82	725	102	4.928
30	5642	57	34.336	83	623	94	4.652
31	5585	57	33.681	84	529	84	4.390
32	5528	56	33.023	85	445	78	4.125
33	5472	55	32.356	86	367	71	3.895
34	5417	55	31.679	87	296	64	3.709
35	5362	55	30.999	88	232	51	3.395
36	5307	56	30.315	89	181	39	3.467
37	5251	57	29.633	90	142	37	3.282
38	5194	58	28.953	91	105	30	3.262
39	5136	61	28.274	92	75	21	3.367
40	5075	66	27.608	93	54	14	3.481
41	5009	69	26.965	94	40	10	3.525
42	4940	71	26.335	95	30	7	3.533
43	4869	71	25.712	96	23	5	3.457
44	4798	71	25.085	97	18	4	3.278
45	4727	70	24.454	98	14	3	3.071
46	4657	69	23.814	99	11	2	2.773
47	4588	67	23.165	100	9	2	2.278
48	4521	63	22.500	101	7	2	1.786
49	4458	61	21.811	102	5	2	1.300
50	4397	59	21.107	103	3	2	0.833
51	4338	62	20.387	104	1	1	0.500
52	4276	65	19.676				

VII. EQUITABLE TABLE (Griffith Davies).

Age.	Living.	Dying.	Expectation.	Age.	Living.	Dying.	Expectation.
10	2844	11	48.83	54	1785	41	18.43
11	2833	11	48.02	55	1744	42	17.85
12	2822	12	47.20	56	1702	43	17.28
13	2810	12	46.40	57	1659	44	16.71
14	2798	13	45.60	58	1615	45	16.15
15	2785	14	44.81	59	1570	46	15.60
16	2771	15	44.04	60	1524	46	15.06
17	2756	16	43.27	61	1478	46	14.51
18	2740	17	42.52	62	1432	47	13.96
19	2723	18	41.78	63	1385	48	13.42
20	2705	18	41.06	64	1337	49	12.88
21	2687	18	40.33	65	1288	50	12.35
22	2669	19	39.60	66	1238	51	11.83
23	2650	19	38.88	67	1187	52	11.32
24	2631	20	38.16	68	1135	53	10.82
25	2611	20	37.44	69	1082	54	10.32
26	2591	21	36.73	70	1028	54	9.84
27	2570	22	36.02	71	974	55	9.36
28	2548	23	35.33	72	919	55	8.88
29	2525	24	34.65	73	864	56	8.42
30	2501	24	33.98	74	808	56	7.97
31	2477	25	33.30	75	752	55	7.52
32	2452	26	32.64	76	697	55	7.08
33	2426	26	31.98	77	642	54	6.64
34	2400	26	31.32	78	588	54	6.20
35	2374	27	30.66	79	534	54	5.78
36	2347	27	30.01	80	480	54	5.38
37	2320	28	29.35	81	426	53	5.00
38	2292	28	28.70	82	373	52	4.63
39	2264	28	28.05	83	321	50	4.30
40	2236	28	27.40	84	271	47	4.00
41	2208	28	26.74	85	224	43	3.73
42	2180	28	26.07	86	181	38	3.50
43	2152	29	25.40	87	143	32	3.31
44	2123	30	24.75	88	111	26	3.11
45	2093	30	24.10	89	85	20	2.91
46	2063	30	23.44	90	65	16	2.65
47	2033	31	22.78	91	49	13	2.36
48	2002	32	22.12	92	36	11	2.03
49	1970	33	21.47	93	25	9	1.70
50	1937	35	20.83	94	16	7	1.31
51	1902	37	20.20	95	9	5	1.05
52	1865	39	19.59	96	4	3	0.75
53	1826	41	19.00	97	1	1	0.50

VIII. COMBINED EXPERIENCE TABLE (Jenkin Jones).

Age.	Living.	Dying.	Expectation.	Age.	Living.	Dying.	Expectation.
10	100000	676	48.36	55	63469	1375	16.86
11	99324	674	47.68	56	62094	1436	16.22
12	98650	672	47.01	57	60658	1497	15.59
13	97978	671	46.33	58	59161	1561	14.97
14	97307	671	45.64	59	57600	1627	14.37
15	96636	671	44.96	60	55973	1698	13.77
16	95965	672	44.27	61	54275	1770	13.18
17	95293	673	43.58	62	52505	1844	12.61
18	94620	675	42.88	63	50661	1917	12.05
19	93945	677	42.19	64	48744	1990	11.51
20	93268	680	41.49	65	46754	2061	10.97
21	92588	683	40.79	66	44693	2128	10.46
22	91905	686	40.09	67	42565	2191	9.96
23	91219	690	39.39	68	40374	2246	9.47
24	90529	694	38.68	69	38128	2291	9.00
25	89835	698	37.98	70	35837	2327	8.54
26	89137	703	37.27	71	33510	2351	8.10
27	88434	708	36.56	72	31159	2362	7.67
28	87726	714	35.86	73	28797	2358	7.26
29	87012	720	35.15	74	26439	2339	6.86
30	86292	727	34.43	75	24100	2303	6.48
31	85565	734	33.72	76	21797	2249	6.11
32	84831	742	33.01	77	19548	2179	5.76
33	84089	750	32.30	78	17369	2092	5.42
34	83339	758	31.58	79	15277	1987	5.09
35	82581	767	30.87	80	13290	1866	4.78
36	81814	776	30.15	81	11424	1730	4.48
37	81038	785	29.44	82	9694	1582	4.18
38	80253	795	28.72	83	8112	1427	3.90
39	79458	805	28.00	84	6685	1268	3.63
40	78653	815	27.28	85	5417	1111	3.36
41	77838	826	26.56	86	4306	958	3.10
42	77012	839	25.84	87	3348	811	2.84
43	76173	857	25.12	88	2537	673	2.59
44	75316	881	24.40	89	1864	545	2.35
45	74435	909	23.69	90	1319	427	2.11
46	73526	944	22.97	91	892	322	1.89
47	72582	981	22.27	92	570	231	1.67
48	71601	1021	21.56	93	339	155	1.47
49	70580	1063	20.87	94	184	95	1.28
50	69517	1108	20.18	95	89	52	1.12
51	68409	1156	19.50	96	37	24	0.99
52	67253	1207	18.82	97	13	9	0.89
53	66046	1261	18.16	98	4	3	0.75
54	64785	1316	17.50	99	1	1	0.50

IX. BELGIAN TABLE (Adolphe Quetelet).

Age.	Living.	Dying.	Expectation.	Age.	Living.	Dying.	Expectation.
0	1000	149	38.18	50	409	8	19.59
1	851	56	43.78	51	401	8	18.97
2	795	31	45.82	52	393	8	18.35
3	764	19	46.64	53	385	8	17.70
4	745	15	46.85	54	377	8	17.06
5	730	10	46.77	55	369	8	16.42
6	720	9	46.44	56	361	8	15.77
7	711	8	46.02	57	353	8	15.12
8	703	6	45.51	58	345	8	14.45
9	697	6	44.93	59	337	9	13.80
10	691	5	44.28	60	328	10	13.16
11	686	4	43.60	61	318	11	12.56
12	682	3	42.95	62	307	12	11.97
13	679	3	42.04	63	295	12	11.43
14	676	3	41.22	64	283	13	10.92
15	673	3	40.40	65	270	13	10.43
16	670	4	39.58	66	257	14	9.93
17	666	5	38.81	67	243	14	9.47
18	661	8	38.10	68	229	14	9.04
19	653	8	37.57	69	215	15	8.60
20	645	8	37.06	70	200	15	7.91
21	637	9	36.51	71	185	15	7.83
22	628	8	36.01	72	170	16	7.57
23	620	8	35.49	73	154	15	7.18
24	612	7	34.92	74	139	15	6.89
25	605	7	34.32	75	124	13	6.69
26	598	7	33.72	76	111	12	6.42
27	591	7	33.11	77	99	11	6.14
28	584	6	32.50	78	88	10	5.86
29	578	7	31.85	79	78	10	5.54
30	571	7	31.24	80	68	9	5.29
31	564	8	30.62	81	59	8	5.01
32	556	8	29.87	82	51	8	4.72
33	548	8	29.49	83	43	7	4.51
34	540	8	28.91	84	36	6	4.22
35	532	8	28.34	85	30	5	3.97
36	524	8	27.74	86	25	5	3.74
37	516	8	27.19	87	20	4	3.45
38	508	8	26.60	88	16	4	3.29
39	500	9	26.03	89	12	3	3.09
40	491	8	25.47	90	9	3	3.11
41	483	8	24.91	91	6	1	3.12
42	475	8	24.27	92	5	1	2.89
43	467	8	23.72	93	4	1	2.52
44	459	8	23.13	94	3	1	2.12
45	451	8	22.53	95	2	0	1.90
46	443	9	21.93	96	2	1	1.71
47	434	9	21.37	97	1	0	1.50
48	425	8	20.79	98	1	1	0.08
49	417	8	20.20	99	0		

X. ENGLISH TABLE No. 1 (William Farr).

Age.	Living.	Dying.	Expectation.	Age.	Living.	Dying.	Expectation.
0	10000	1463	41.17	51	4586	75	19.83
1	8536	526	47.17	52	4511	76	19.17
2	8010	271	49.17	53	4434	76	18.50
3	7739	185	49.92	54	4358	78	17.83
4	7553	133	50.08	55	4279	84	17.17
5	7420	104	50.00	56	4194	90	16.50
6	7315	83	49.75	57	4103	96	15.83
7	7232	67	49.25	58	4007	101	15.17
8	7164	56	48.75	59	3906	106	14.58
9	7108	46	48.08	60	3799	112	14.00
10	7061	39	47.42	61	3687	117	13.42
11	7022	36	46.75	62	3569	123	12.83
12	6985	35	46.00	63	3446	128	12.25
13	6950	41	45.17	64	3318	133	11.75
14	6909	46	44.42	65	3185	138	11.17
15	6862	49	43.65	66	3046	142	10.67
16	6813	50	43.00	67	2904	147	10.17
17	6762	51	42.34	68	2759	150	9.67
18	6710	52	41.67	69	2606	153	9.25
19	6658	52	41.00	70	2453	156	8.75
20	6605	53	40.34	71	2297	157	8.34
21	6552	54	39.67	72	2139	158	7.92
22	6497	55	39.00	73	1981	158	7.50
23	6442	56	38.34	74	1823	156	7.08
24	6386	56	37.67	75	1666	154	6.75
25	6329	57	37.00	76	1512	151	6.42
26	6271	58	36.34	77	1360	146	6.00
27	6213	59	35.67	78	1214	140	5.67
28	6154	60	35.00	79	1073	134	5.34
29	6094	60	34.34	80	939	126	5.08
30	6033	61	33.67	81	813	117	4.75
31	5971	62	33.00	82	696	108	4.50
32	5909	63	32.34	83	588	98	4.25
33	5845	63	31.67	84	490	87	4.00
34	5782	64	31.08	85	402	77	3.75
35	5717	65	30.42	86	324	67	3.50
36	5651	66	29.75	87	257	57	3.34
37	5585	66	29.08	88	200	47	3.08
38	5518	67	28.42	89	152	38	2.92
39	5451	68	27.75	90	114	32	2.75
40	5382	69	27.17	91	82	24	2.58
41	5313	69	26.50	92	58	18	2.42
42	5243	70	25.83	93	40	13	2.34
43	5173	71	25.17	94	27	10	2.17
44	5102	71	24.50	95	17	6	2.08
45	5030	72	23.83	96	11	5	1.20
46	4957	73	23.17	97	6	2	1.16
47	4884	73	22.50	98	4	2	1.00
48	4811	74	21.83	99	2	1	0.75
49	4736	74	21.17	100	1	1	0.00
50	4662	75	20.58	101	0		

XI. ENGLISH TABLE No. 2 (William Farr).

Age.	Living.	Dying.	Expectation.	Age.	Living.	Dying.	Expectation.
0	5126235	817331	40.36	55	2147180	47003	16.66
1	4308904	281493	46.95	56	2100177	48530	16.02
2	4027411	145352	49.20	57	2051647	51921	15.39
3	3882059	95786	50.03	58	1999726	55033	14.77
4	3786273	69451	50.28	59	1944693	57914	14.18
5	3716822	50073	50.21	60	1886779	60599	13.60
6	3666749	36653	49.89	61	1826180	63119	13.03
7	3630096	31331	49.39	62	1763061	65497	12.48
8	3598765	26047	48.81	63	1697564	67744	11.94
9	3572718	22976	48.16	64	1629820	69861	11.42
10	3549742	19260	47.47	65	1559959	71841	10.90
11	3530482	16926	46.73	66	1488118	73663	10.41
12	3513556	16658	45.95	67	1414455	75302	9.92
13	3496888	16496	45.17	68	1339153	76718	9.45
14	3480392	19061	44.38	69	1262435	77871	9.00
15	3461331	17203	43.62	70	1184564	78709	8.55
16	3444128	19532	42.84	71	1105855	79182	8.13
17	3424596	22674	42.08	72	1026673	79234	7.72
18	3401922	25802	41.35	73	947439	78817	7.32
19	3376120	26861	40.67	74	868622	77884	6.94
20	3349259	27125	39.99	75	790738	76400	6.57
21	3322134	27380	39.31	76	714338	74342	6.22
22	3294754	27629	38.63	77	639996	71704	5.89
23	3267125	27879	37.96	78	568292	68499	5.57
24	3239246	28128	37.28	79	499793	64759	5.26
25	3211118	28383	36.60	80	435034	60540	4.97
26	3182735	28647	35.92	81	374494	55914	4.70
27	3154088	28924	35.24	82	318580	50979	4.44
28	3125164	29215	34.57	83	267601	45839	4.19
29	3095949	29525	33.89	84	221762	40614	3.96
30	3066424	29856	33.21	85	181148	35425	3.74
31	3036568	30208	32.53	86	145723	30387	3.53
32	3006360	30585	31.85	87	115336	25611	3.33
33	2975775	30990	31.17	88	89725	21186	3.14
34	2944785	31420	30.50	89	68539	17184	2.97
35	2913365	31886	29.82	90	51355	13652	2.80
36	2881479	32379	29.15	91	37703	10611	2.65
37	2849100	32905	28.47	92	27092	8060	2.50
38	2816195	33464	27.80	93	19032	5977	2.36
39	2782731	34053	27.13	94	13055	4321	2.23
40	2748678	34678	26.46	95	8734	3043	2.11
41	2714000	35334	25.79	96	5691	2083	2.00
42	2678666	36024	25.12	97	3608	1385	1.89
43	2642642	36743	24.46	98	2222	894	1.79
44	2605899	37495	23.79	99	1328	559	1.69
45	2568404	38272	23.13	100	769	338	
46	2530132	39077	22.48	101	431	198	
47	2491055	39908	21.82	102	233	111	
48	2451147	40759	21.17	103	122	61	
49	2410388	41629	20.52	104	61	31	
50	2368759	42514	19.87	105	30	16	
51	2326245	43412	19.22	106	14	8	
52	2282833	44315	18.58	107	6	3	
53	2238518	45219	17.94	108	3	2	
54	2193299	46119	17.30	109	1	1	

XII. FARR'S ENGLISH TABLE No. 3.—MALES.*

Age.	Living.	Dying.	Expectation.	Age.	Living.	Dying.	Expectation.
0	511745	83719	39.91	55	209539	5144	16.45
1	428026	27521	46.65	56	204395	5281	15.86
2	400505	14215	48.83	57	199114	5428	15.26
3	386290	9213	49.61	58	193686	5584	14.68
4	377077	6719	49.81	59	188102	5752	14.10
5	370358	5033	49.71	60	182350	5929	13.53
6	363325	3953	49.39	61	176421	6118	12.96
7	361372	3310	48.92	62	170303	6314	12.41
8	358062	2734	48.37	63	163989	6515	11.87
9	355328	2297	47.74	64	157474	6720	11.34
10	553031	1983	47.05	65	150754	6921	10.82
11	351048	1776	46.31	66	143833	7115	10.32
12	349272	1666	45.54	67	136718	7297	9.83
13	347606	1637	44.76	68	129421	7458	8.36
14	345969	1679	43.97	69	121963	7593	8.90
15	344290	1781	43.18	70	114370	7695	8.45
16	342509	1928	42.40	71	106675	7756	8.03
17	340581	2112	41.64	72	98919	7770	7.62
18	338469	2320	40.90	73	91149	7733	7.22
19	336149	2541	40.17	74	83416	7639	6.85
20	333608	2764	39.48	75	75777	7483	6.49
21	330844	2801	38.80	76	68294	7268	6.15
22	328043	2836	38.13	77	61026	6990	5.82
23	325207	2868	37.46	78	54036	6655	5.51
24	322339	2897	36.79	79	47381	6266	5.21
25	319442	2926	36.12	80	41115	5832	4.93
26	316516	2954	35.44	81	35283	5361	4.66
27	313562	2981	34.77	82	29922	4862	4.41
28	310581	3009	34.10	83	25060	4349	4.17
29	307572	3038	33.43	84	20711	3834	3.95
30	304534	3068	32.76	85	16877	3328	3.73
31	301466	3100	32.09	86	13549	2840	3.53
32	298366	3134	31.42	87	10709	2384	3.34
33	295232	3171	30.74	88	8325	1965	3.16
34	292061	3211	30.07	89	6360	1590	3.00
35	288850	3254	29.40	90	4770	1260	2.84
36	285596	3300	28.73	91	3510	979	2.69
37	282296	3352	28.06	92	2531	744	2.55
38	278944	3406	27.39	93	1787	553	2.41
39	275538	3465	26.72	94	1234	401	2.29
40	272073	3529	26.06	95	833	285	2.17
41	268544	3596	25.39	96	548	196	2.06
42	264948	3668	54.73	97	352	132	1.95
43	261280	3746	24.07	98	220	86	1.85
44	257534	3826	23.41	99	134	55	1.76
45	253708	3912	22.76	100	79	33	1.68
46	249796	4001	22.11	101	46	21	
47	245795	4095	21.46	102	25	11	
48	241700	4192	20.82	103	14	7	
49	237508	4292	20.17	104	7	3	
50	233216	4395	19.54	105	4	2	
51	228821	4626	18.90	106	2	1	
52	254195	4758	18.28	107	1	1	
53	219437	4885	17.67	108	0	0	
54	214552	5013	17.06	109			

* Dr. Farr's English Life, Males, No. 3, has recently been adopted by the Legislature of New York as the basis of annual valuations of life policies by the New York Insurance Department—interest assumed at 5 per cent.

TABLE OF HEIGHT AND WEIGHT.*

The following table shows what the best authorities regard as the most desirable Proportion of the Height of Individuals to their Weight.

HEIGHT.		WEIGHT.
Ft.	In.	Lbs.
5	1	120
5	2	125
5	3	130
5	4	135
5	5	140
5	6	143
5	7	145
5	8	148
5	9	155
5	10	160
5	11	165
6	00	170

* Compiled by Minturn Post, M. D., and Isaac L. Kip, M. D., Medical Examiners to the Mutual Life Insurance Company of New York, from observations upon the proper proportions of height and weight among *American* lives. This differs slightly from the English standards. It is substantially the same as those adopted by most of the American companies. Of course it is not expected that this proportion be *adhered* to in taking risks. It is only considered as the most *desirable* proportion.

SHORT RULE FOR EXPECTATION.

It may be convenient to know the expectation of life when one cannot have access to the tables. Either of the following simple rules, though only an approximate estimate, will give a result sufficiently accurate for ordinary purposes:

From **14** to **25** inclusive deduct the age from **100**; half the balance is the Expectation.
" **26** " **30** " " **98** " "
" **31** " **40** " " **96** " "
" **41** " **50** " " **92** " "
" **51** " **60** " " **90** " "

Or deduct the age of the party, whatever it may be, from 80, and two-thirds of the difference is the Expectation.

DISCOUNT TABLE.*

Present Value of One Dollar, due at the end of any number of Years not exceeding 100.

End of Year.	4 per Cent.	5 per Cent.	6 per Cent.	End of Year.	4 per Cent.	5 per Cent.	6 per Cent.
1	.961538	.952381	.943396	51	.135301	.083051	.051215
2	.924556	.907029	.889996	52	.130097	.079096	.048316
3	.888996	.863838	.839619	53	.125093	.075330	.045582
4	.854804	.822702	.792094	54	.120282	.071743	.043001
5	.821927	.783526	.747258	55	.115656	.068326	.040567
6	.790315	.746215	.704961	56	.111207	.065073	.038271
7	.759918	.710681	.665057	57	.106930	.061974	.036105
8	.730690	.676839	.627412	58	.102817	.059023	.034061
9	.702587	.644609	.591898	59	.098863	.056212	.032133
10	.675564	.613913	.588395	60	.095060	.053536	.030314
11	.649581	.584679	.526788	61	.091404	.050986	.028598
12	.624597	.556837	.496969	62	.087889	.048558	.026980
13	.600574	.530321	.468839	63	.084508	.046246	.025453
14	.577475	.505068	.442301	64	.081258	.044044	.024012
15	.555265	.481017	.417265	65	.078133	.041946	.022653
16	.533908	.458112	.393646	66	.075128	.039949	.021370
17	.513373	.436297	.371364	67	.072238	.038047	.020161
18	.493628	.415521	.350344	68	.069460	.036235	.019020
19	.474642	.395734	.330513	69	.066788	.034509	.018943
20	.456387	.376889	.311805	70	.064219	.032866	.016927
21	.438834	.358942	.294155	71	.061749	.031301	.015969
22	.421955	.341850	.277505	72	.059374	.029811	.015065
23	.405726	.325571	.261797	73	.057091	.028391	.014213
24	.390121	.310068	.246979	74	.054895	.027039	.013408
25	.375117	.295303	.232999	75	.052784	.025752	.012649
26	.360689	.281241	.219810	76	.050754	.024525	.011933
27	.346817	.267848	.207368	77	.048801	.023353	.011258
28	.333477	.255094	.195630	78	.046924	.022245	.010620
29	.320651	.242946	.184557	79	.045120	.021186	.010019
30	.308319	.231377	.174110	80	.043384	.020177	.009452
31	.296460	.220359	.164255	81	.041716	.019216	.008917
32	.285058	.209866	.154957	82	.040111	.018301	.008412
33	.274094	.199873	.146186	83	.038569	.017430	.007936
34	.263552	.190355	.137912	84	.037085	.016600	.007487
35	.253415	.181290	.130105	85	.035659	.015809	.007063
36	.243669	.172657	.122741	86	.034287	.015056	.006663
37	.234297	.164436	.115793	87	.032969	.014339	.006286
38	.225285	.156605	.109239	88	.031701	.013657	.005930
39	.216621	.149148	.103056	89	.030481	.013006	.005595
40	.208289	.142046	.097222	90	.029309	.012387	.005278
41	.200278	.135282	.091719	91	.028182	.011797	.004979
42	.192575	.128840	.086527	92	.027098	.011235	.004697
43	.185168	.122704	.081630	93	.026056	.010700	.004432
44	.178046	.116861	.077009	94	.025053	.010191	.004181
45	.171198	.111297	.072650	95	.024090	.009705	.003944
46	.164614	.105997	.068538	96	.023163	.009243	.003721
47	.158283	.100949	.064658	97	.022272	.008803	.003510
48	.152195	.096142	.060998	98	.021416	.008384	.003312
49	.146341	.091564	.057546	99	.020592	.007985	.003124
50	.140713	.087204	.054288	100	.019800	.007604	.002947

* This Table shows the present value of future payments of One Dollar for any number of years to 100, and will prove useful both to the student of the science and to the solicitor.

COMPARATIVE MORTALITY TABLE—I.

Showing how many Persons will survive each Year out of the number starting in the Year of life indicated by the several Tables.

Age.	Dr. Farr's English Life. Male No. 3.	Actuaries.	Adjusted Experience of Mut. Life.*	Age.	Dr. Farr's English Life. Male No. 3.	Actuaries.	Adjusted Experience of Mut. Life.*
0	511,745			55	209,539	63,469	65,208
1	428,026			56	204,395	62,094	64,122
2	400,505			57	199,114	60,658	62,991
3	386,290			58	193,686	59,161	61,806
4	377,077			59	188,102	57,600	60,559
5	370,358			60	182,350	55,973	59,242
6	365,325			61	176,421	54,275	57,843
7	361,372			62	170,303	52,505	56,358
8	358,062			63	163,989	50,661	54,780
9	355,328			64	157,474	48,744	53,105
10	353,031	100,000	100,000	65	150,754	46,754	51,331
11	351,048	99,324	99,259	66	143,833	44,693	49,453
12	349,372	98,650	98,520	67	136,718	42,565	47,475
13	347,606	97,978	97,782	68	129,421	40,374	45,393
14	345,969	97,307	97,045	69	121,963	38,128	43,200
15	344,290	96,636	96,309	70	114,370	35,837	40,896
16	342,509	95,965	95,574	71	106,675	33,510	38,469
17	340,581	95,293	94,840	72	98,919	31,159	35,930
18	338,469	94,620	94,107	73	91,149	28,797	33,307
19	336,149	93,945	93,375	74	83,416	26,439	30,577
20	333,608	93,268	92,644	75	75,777	24,100	......
21	330,844	92,588	91,912	76	68,294	21,797	......
22	328,043	91,905	91,180	77	61,026	19,548	......
23	325,207	91.219	90,447	78	54,036	17,369	......
24	322,339	90,529	89,714	79	47,381	15,277	17,669
25	319,442	89,835	88,980	80	41,115	13,290	......
26	316,516	89,137	88,245	81	35,283	11,424	......
27	313,562	88,434	87,510	82	29,922	9,694	......
28	310,581	87,726	86,774	83	25,060	8,112	......
29	307,572	87,012	86,037	84	20,711	6,685	7,732
30	304,534	86,292	85,299	85	16,877	5,417	......
31	301,466	85,565	84,561	86	13,549	4,306	......
32	298,366	84,831	83,822	87	10,709	3,348	......
33	295,232	84,089	83,083	88	8,325	2,537	......
34	292,061	83,339	82,343	89	6,360	1,864	2,156
35	288,850	82,581	81,603	90	4,770	1,319	......
36	285,596	81,814	80,863	91	3,510	892	......
37	282,296	81,038	80,123	92	2,531	570	......
38	278,944	80,253	79,385	93	1,787	339	......
39	275,538	79,458	78,649	94	1,234	184	213
40	272,073	78,653	77,917	95	833	89	......
41	268,544	77,838	77,191	96	548	37	......
42	264,948	77,012	76,470	97	352	13	......
43	261,280	76,173	75,753	98	220	4	......
44	257,534	75,316	75,034	99	134	1	1
45	253,708	74,435	74,305	100	79	0	0
46	249,796	73,526	73,555	101	46		
47	245,795	72,582	72,771	102	25		
48	241,700	71,601	71,947	103	14		
49	237,508	70,580	71,080	104	7		
50	233,216	69,517	70,172	105	4		
51	228,821	68,409	69,231	106	2		
52	224,195	67,253	68,265	107	1		
53	219,437	66,046	67,275	108	0		
54	214,552	64,785	66,257				

* This does not by any means give the exact mortality experienced by the Mutual Life Insurance Company.

COMPARATIVE MORTALITY TABLE—II.*

Showing the number expected to die out of 1,000 persons entering each year, according to three English and one American Experience Tables; also, in the fifth column, the number actually dying, as proven by the Massachusetts Commissioners' observations among insured lives during seven years—1859 to 1865.

Age.	English Life. No. 3.	Carlisle.	Actuaries.	Mutual Life. General Experience.	Massachusetts Experience. 7 years.
25	9.20	7.31	7.77	8.26	7.01
26	9.38	7.36	7.88	8.33	6.69
27	9.55	7.76	8.00	8.41	6.59
28	9.74	8.69	8.13	8.49	6.74
29	9.93	9.82	8.27	8.57	6.80
30	10.13	10.10	8.42	8.66	7.42
31	10.34	10.20	8.57	8.74	8.01
32	10.56	10.13	8.74	8.82	6.76
33	10.80	10.05	8.91	8.91	6.05
34	11.05	10.15	9.09	8.99	8.14
35	11.33	10.25	9.28	9.07	7.43
36	11.62	10.55	9.48	9.15	6.34
37	11.94	10.85	9.68	9.21	6.56
38	12.29	11.16	9.90	9.27	8.12
39	12.65	11.87	16.13	9.31	8.51
40	13.06	13.05	10.36	9.32	8.68
41	13.48	13.77	10.61	9.34	7.83
42	13.94	14.37	10.89	9.38	8.40
43	14.44	14.58	11.25	9.49	7.09
44	14.97	14.79	11.69	9.72	9.49
45	15.54	14.80	12.21	10.10	8.53
46	16.15	14.81	12.83	10.66	9.74
47	16.18	14.60	13.51	11.33	9.19
48	17.49	13.93	14.25	12.05	10.28
49	18.23	13.68	15.06	12.77	9.59
50	19.02	13.41	15.93	13.41	9.73
51	20.42	14.29	16.89	13.95	10.14
52	21.45	15.20	17.94	14.51	10.63
53	22.51	16.14	19.09	15.13	13.13
54	23.64	16.89	20.31	15.83	14.34
55	24.85	17.92	21.66	16.66	12.07
56	26.17	19.00	23.12	17.64	13.30
57	27.63	20.89	24.67	18.81	16.46
58	29.25	24.20	26.38	20.17	17.04
59	31.05	28.27	28 24	21.75	19.77
60	33.05	33.48	30.33	23.61	20.95
61	35.29	35.78	32.61	25.68	20.79
62	37.77	37.40	35.12	28.00	18.92
63	40.53	38.25	37.83	30.57	27.48
64	43.60	39.77	40.82	33.40	25.55
65	46.98	41.08	44.08	36.59	35.13
66	50.71	42.50	47.61	40.00	30.07
67	54.83	44.38	51.47	43.86	40.15
68	59.33	46.45	55.63	48.31	42.65
69	64.25	49.10	60.08	53.33	33.05
70	69.62	51.64	64.93	59.35	68.00
99		1000.00	1000.00	1000.00	

* As it will be interesting and instructive still farther to show the results of observations upon AMERICAN lives, in comparison with other calculations made in England, we append two other Comparative Mortality Tables.

COMPARATIVE MORTALITY TABLE—III.

Showing the number of deaths in the year following each year of age from twenty-five to seventy inclusive, out of one thousand persons living at each of such ages, according to the experience of the three several Tables of mortality known as the *Carlisle*, the *Actuaries'* or *Combined Experience*, and the *English Life*, compared with Mutual Benefit Tables.

Persons Living.	AGE.	Deaths in next y'r Mutual Benefit.	Deaths in next year Carlisle.	Deaths in next year Actuaries'.	Deaths in next year English Life.
1000	25	4.24	7.31	7.77	9.20
1000	26	10.29	7.36	7.88	9.38
1000	27	9.91	7.76	8.00	9.55
1000	28	8.42	8.69	8.13	9.74
1000	29	8.32	9.82	8.27	9.93
1000	30	6.98	10.10	8.42	10.13
1000	31	8.28	10.20	8.57	10.34
1000	32	9.80	10.13	8.74	10.56
1000	33	8.18	10.05	8.91	10.80
1000	34	9.71	10.15	9.09	11.05
1000	35	7.52	10.25	9.28	11.33
1000	36	8.69	10.55	9.48	11.62
1000	37	9.74	10.85	9.68	11.94
1000	38	8.91	11.16	9.90	12.29
1000	39	10.21	11.87	10.13	12.65
1000	40	7.58	13.05	10.36	13.06
1000	41	12.01	13.77	10.61	13.48
1000	42	8.24	14.37	10.89	13.94
1000	43	12.03	14.58	11.25	14.44
1000	44	11.38	14.79	11.69	14.97
1000	45	10.11	14.80	12.21	15.54
1000	46	8.33	14.81	12.83	16.15
1000	47	12.63	14.60	13.51	16.80
1000	48	12.60	13.93	14.25	17.49
1000	49	11.13	13.68	15.06	18.23
1000	50	16.30	13.41	15.93	19.02
1000	51	14.09	14.29	16.89	20.42
1000	52	11.25	15.20	17.94	21.45
1000	53	19.50	16.14	19.09	22.51
1000	54	15.27	16.89	20.31	23.64
1000	55	12.95	17.92	21.66	24.85
1000	56	20.69	19.00	23.12	26.17
1000	57	21.76	20.89	24.67	27.63
1000	58	19.58	24.20	26.38	29.25
1000	59	21.13	28.27	28.24	31.05
1000	60	26.67	33.48	30.33	33.05
1000	61	28.24	35.78	32.61	35.29
1000	62	26.03	37.40	35.12	37.77
1000	63	17.76	38.25	37.83	40.53
1000	64	17.59	39.77	40.82	43.60
1000	65	16.55	41.08	44.08	46.98
1000	66	40.98	42.50	47.61	50.71
1000	67	34.31	44.38	51.47	54.83
1000	68	53.89	46.45	55.63	59.33
1000	69	23.08	49.10	60.08	64.25
1000	70	26.78	51.64	64.93	69.62

ORIGIN AND BUSINESS OF COMPANIES,

IN ***NEW POLICIES,*** (1st line) TOTAL ***INCOME,*** (2d line) AND TOTAL ***ASSETS,*** (3d line)

COMPILED FROM ORIGINAL SOURCES EXPRESSLY FOR THIS WORK.

FROM 1843 TO 1866.

	1843.	**1844.**	**1845.**	**1846.**	**1847.**	**1848.**
Mutual of New York	476	616	1,047 $215,571 68	1,085 $322,557 87	1,466 † $812,230 80 † $550,298 56	1,505 $333,912 04 $758,473 14
New England Mutual		343 $25,697 00 $18,626 00	459 49,112 00 63,369 00	435 72,209 00 104,313 00	461 94,147 00 170,339 00	413 106,936 00 223,995 00
Mutual Benefit			693	2,316 264,661 31 198,724 51	1,847 308,923 71 444,314 82	1,406 345,810 51 673,362 96
New York Life			449 22,688 64	632 48,012 05	796 73,626 93	1,821 149,624 26 114,437 58
State Mutual			530 16,703 26 ‡ 66,703 26	439 30,653 67 97,356 93	538 49,220 50 146,577 43	376 39,244 16 176,853 59
Connecticut Mutual					892 58,416 00 92,612 00	2,751 187,142 00 184,959 00

	1849.	1850.	1851.	1852.	1853.	1854.
Union Mutual	Organized.	1,546	2,259	1,783	902	547
		$182,895 23	$173,169 09	$177,310 39	$182,758 81	$169,903 11
United States		408	539	1,161	575	422
		31,651 00	51,417 00	90,457 00	100,802 00	103,424 00
		117,980 00	142,551 00	178,063 00	206,211 00	238,684 00
Manhattan			953	964	626	611
		Organized.	71,515 17	97,922 48	98,149 48	148,332 38
			140,773 97	196,863 51	246,532 13	319,721 93
National, Vermont		384	281	184	272	180
		14,216 41	20,080 61	24,813 12	31,999 75	32,558 28
		8,645 62	16,177 17	28,087 75	44,741 54	62,027 84
Charter Oak						
		Organized		54,750 29	59,986 33	95,292 51
Ætna						
		Organized.				
Phœnix Mutual				335	513	923
			Organized	9,762 60	23,723 43	34,676 41
Berkshire				112	192	455
			Organized.	4,312 31	10,200 36	28,441 39

† Total for the five years, 1843 to 1847 inclusive. ‡ This includes Guarantee Capital.

ORIGIN AND BUSINESS OF COMPANIES—CONTINUED.

	1849.	1850.	1851.	1852.	1853.	1854.
Massachusetts Mutual			Organized.	312	223	202
				$11,532 22	$12,696 06	$17,326 37
				*$105,031 45	$108,397 20	$116,704 79
Knickerbocker					393	276
					†23,839 16	39,104 84
					127,152 10	14,070 74
Mutual of New York	1,755	1,363	978	1,060	1,260	1,568
	$471,189 39	$530,906 38	$544,601 16	688,123 46	776,227 61	780,798 71
	$1,000,439 62	$1,280,088 46	$1,592,655 56	2,018,775 61	2,444,684 81	2,734,485 31
New England Mutual	557	335	343	488	502	453
	130,220 00	145,668 00	146,197 00	167,992 00	190,812 00	220,780 00
	258,673 00	344,611 00	433,416 00	539,301 00	‡649,380 00	629,827 00
Mutual Benefit	1,509	747	499	496	512	463
	498,018 21	538,361 55	526,679 50	551,839 40	574,277 40	597,144 27
	935,944 96	1,192,441 66	1,381,008 64	1,559,092 12	1,774,005 46	2,033,859 47
New York Life	1,069	1,755	1,329	1,260	639	485
	129,821 36	275,809 47	321,782 72	356,242 47	384,558 40	367,357 65
	164,368 88	320,581 27	354,755 24	456,751 00	636,678 92	814,044 95
State Mutual	315	189	275	361	227	141
	60,572 17	51,275 51	60,573 17	59,828 00	69,064 96	50,272 44
	194,426 91	212,863 92	186,148 29	197,503 88	228,982 91	250,631 31
Connecticut Mutual	4,243	5,589	2,699	1,320	935	939
	422,225 00	693,905 00	742,816 00	741,172 00	737,178 00	769,068 00
	469,803 00	918,406 00	1,351,036 00	1,701,673 00	1,980,170 00	2,154,489 00

	1855.	1856.	1857.	1858.	1859.	1860.
Mutual of New York	1,698 $880,916 35 $3,178,034 28	2,041 $1,045,235 17 $3,787,945 76	1,863 $1,166,732 97 $4,488,043 99	1,728 $1,305,604 70 $5,188,933 42	1,721 $1,445,951 97 $6,013,855 20	1,701 $1,539,575 75 $6,989,856 74
New England Mutual	516 249,104 00 768,984 00	666 299,390 00 964,418 00	532 330,568 00 1,144,856 00	826 417,844 00 ‡1,395,622 00	1,007 467,508 00 1,342,856 00	1,388 580,805 00 1,706,700 00
Mutual Benefit	446 626,315 35 2,230,005 47	473 645,366 27 2,484,512 18	587 695,017 99 2,743,325 73	913 759,853 36 3,001,920 91	1,366 876,817 53 3,400,582 39	1,435 977,067 74 3,812,558 50
New York Life	474 378,186 14 902,062 70	706 408,223 27 1,509,008 65	711 474,191 32 1,191,545 59	626 495,761 20 1,402,966 25	887 564,384 22 1,595,901 56	1,024 608,639 45 1,767,133 24
State Mutual	134 62,985 05 280,760 33	177 63,786 70 320,867 40	256 69,877 56 393,573 59	175 69,009 21 437,580 67	192 75,381 61 477,619 29	198 84,008 21 529,735 63
Connecticut Mutual	692 766,963 00 2,271,837 00	587 776,418 00 2,473,037 00	565 802,804 00 2,706,765 00	930 853,665 00 3,000,523 00	1,254 946,822 00 3,370,001 00	1,725 1,077,138 00 3,889,411 00
Union Mutual	376 150,118 87	341 139,517 57	236 151,756 33	363 155,799 68	526 165,170 73	505 178,248 12 ....

* These include the Capital (guarantee) of $100,000. † Only the net income is given in years up to 1859.

‡ Including surplus distributed in 1853, '58, '63, and '66.

ORIGIN AND BUSINESS OF COMPANIES—CONTINUED.

	1855.	1856.	1857.	1858.	1859.	1860.
United States	504	1,277	1,004	814	808	1,039
	$123,835 00	$150,926 00	$184,899 00	$196,221 00	$ 207,006 00	$241,274 00
	$283,131 00	$341,324 00	$420,483 00	$497,290 00	$ 576,664 00	$701,482 00
Manhattan	454	682	750	844	1,025	949
	194,030 80	229,531 83	317,105 88	324,811 76	351,701 78	472,368 62
	380,566 67	498,534 96	606,509 27	708,684 76	871,008 07	1,039,820 96
National, Vermont	154	326	299	176	255	281
	32,867 29	43,237 30	50,393 14	54,532 92	61,772 90	77,395 18
	75,156 58	100,032 14	122,915 27	155,994 20	195,758 57	228,164 76
Charter Oak	....	....	....	....	....	....
	127,277 00	136,197 99	139,866 24	205,810 92	260,157 21	277,166 12
	....	....	....	....	....	....
Ætna	....	....	....	....	....	....
	....	....	....	....	....	....
	....	....	....	....	....	....
Phœnix Mutual	631	638	829	490	516	510
	44,160 28	50,373 96	58,815 48	59,332 60	58,946 12	57,999 21
	....	....	....	....	....	....
Berkshire	265	334	274	148	212	324
	33,740 91	43,083 77	50,456 15	47,275 57	54,373 67	65,756 30
	....	....	....	....	....	....
Massachusetts Mutual	339	409	388	384	822	890
	29,683 01	43,802 91	56,446 43	71,570 55	114,828 87	152,280 97
	126,233 85	150,475 05	184,202 10	220,960 31	271,298 12	343,313 42

Knickerbocker	160	174	167	253	319	357
	37,753 05	42,139 56	42,987 01	50,252 42	77,272 31	78,199 78
	150,262 95	171,312 71	188,309 76	209,341 60	233,027 87	263,508 20
Northwestern	....	....	....	....	Organized.	....
	....	....	....	....		....
	....	....	....	....		....
Equitable	....	....	....	....	* 277	609
	....	....	....	....	26,444 00	76,070 00
	....	....	....	....	120,772 00	162,618 00
Guardian	....	....	....	....	147	383
	....	....	....	....	13,736 08	31,590 10
	....	....	....	....	137,115 71	142,516 42
Washington	....	....	....	....	....	328
	....	....	....	....	....	28,298 60
	....	....	....	....	....	141,279 58
Home	....	....	....	....	....	†447
	....	....	....	....	....	39,545 00
	....	....	....	....	....	157,878 00
Germania	....	....	....	....	....	169
	....	....	....	....	....	9,757 22
	....	....	....	....	....	194,545 47

* Five months. † Eight months.

ORIGIN AND BUSINESS OF COMPANIES—CONTINUED.

	1861.	1862.	1863.	1864.	1865.	1866.
Mutual of New York	1,221 $1,593,732 14 $7,839,768 12	1,833 $1,755,285 51 $8,918,167 95	2,842 $2,091,301 62 $10,029,264 81	4,216 $2,849,866 50 $11,790,414 68	8,600 $3,853,065 80 $14,112,249 85	15,258 $6,217,035 88 $17,639,296 97
New England Mutual	1,000 634,707 00 2,043,904 00	1,364 737,363 00 2,372,946 00	1,607 814,222 00 * 2,798,239 00	1,750 1,102 316 00 2,651,116 00	2,399 1,318,271 00 3,362,986 80	4,649 * 1,873,406,00 * 4,508,876 00
Mutual Benefit	894 950,638 20 4,109,353 45	1,740 1,104,955 59 4,439,231 77	3,511 1,528,791 44 5,285,736 00	7,092 2,486,706 56 6,774,867 60	6,819 3,502,839 00 9,049,539 60	7,193 4,034,355 39 11,627,984 73
New York Life	1,201 612,549 80 2,004,857 53	3,302 894,280 99 2,586,246 07	4,675 1,162,191 19 2,705,666 74	4,905 1,729,811 17 3,741,078 48	5,138 2,342,065 40 5,018,449 06	7,296 3,088,804 47 7,009,092 25
State Mutual	129 87,928 82 571,038 20	109 91,602 64 593,797 17	239 105,668 64 639,525 08	304 130,035 13 711,472 29	304 129,436 58 669,399 08	… … …
Connecticut Mutual	1,156 1,117,500 00 4,358,009 00	2,285 1,345,477 00 5,008,849 00	5,672 1,809,713 00 6,030,544 00	8,811 2,938,562 00 7,918,896 00	10,063 4,174,245 00 10,104,209 00	14,138 † 5,339,535 00 ‡ 13,316,275 00
Union Mutual	436 179,827 46 …	334 180,840 14 …	1,030 246,319 18 852,088 41	1,834 398,720 61 1,094,609 43	2,593 394,042 81 1,530,877 17	3,228 1,077,833 00 2,188,429 20
United States	710 237,754 00 804,852 00	665 257,079 00 876,067 00	1,085 314,470 00 1,052,011 00	1,315 424,682 00 1,304,828 00	1,320 540,578 00 1,600,139 00	1,958 713,060 00 2,005,702 09

	812	1,146	1,664	2,140	2,555	3,717
Manhattan	493,549 03	539,567 36	752,401 38	973,534 02	1,281,597 21	1,710,635 00
	1,174,800 40	1,350,467 28	1,548,849 22	1,991,225 23	2,619,190 80	3,525,877 00
	128	170	248	468	461	450
National, Vermont	68,361 13	79,943 49	88,348 54	115,832 47	139,118 55	163,094 02
	254,706 88	292,549 07	348,591 69	405,034 91	439,127 48	524,928 42
	...	9	921	2,245	4,946	834
Charter Oak	230,167 38	...	247,888 54	447,591 33	571,978 80	1,742,844 00
	...	...	657,387 29	948,215 81	1,482,701 84	2,580,049 00
	589	804	1,822	4,577	8,815	14,189
Ætna	78,533 67	94,878 07	199,952 40	980,755 52	1,686,813 61	3,521,930 80
	281,263 65	310,492 04	431,236 02	881,578 72	2,036,823 05	4,401,833 86
	426	604	918	2,297	4,302	...
Phœnix Mutual	59,453 83	74,300 77	118,820 58	183,051 89	379,706 39	848 607
	...	...	353,993 94	472,355 15	819,284 71	1,457,314 00
	237	149	107	308	388	589
Berkshire	70,220 48	75,024 66	92,850 54	135,710 65	140,400 24	273,203 00
	...	317,545 54	...	390,004 41	506,014 46	677,898 00
	821	603	771	1,388	2,478	3,107
Massachusetts Mutual	183,684 79	200,362 97	246,532 02	346,251 51	536,331 07	761,776 81
	440,581 08	475,094 58	604,898 41	742,990 98	1,111,910 62	1,597,565 43
	306	55	886	1,249	2,447	5,422
Knickerbocker	72,500 74	92,624 19	158,146,53	229,709 89	293,253 49	953,982 00
	272,481 72	291,695 92	394,309 83	547,561 56	853,709 10	1,579,145 00

Including surplus distributed in 1853, '58, '63, and '66. † For eleven months only, to 31st December. ‡ December 31.

ORIGIN AND BUSINESS OF COMPANIES—CONTINUED.

	1861.	1862.	1863.	1864.	1865.	1866.
Equitable	678	1,230	1,601	2,844	3,268	7,245
	$103,429 00	$181,378 00	$308,060 00	$579,079 00	$971,505 00	$2,069,070 00
	$210,636 00	$332,298 00	$584,714 00	$1,017,977 00	$1,648,486 00	$3,077,788 00
Guardian	257	688	1,048	1,900	2,804	2,192
	41,322 05	61,821 35	117.291 39	265,532 62	413,305 53	582,610 37
	163,151 90	184,234 63	210,266 44	335,817 17	513,818 13	737,413 66
Washington	225	362	512	919	1,306	1,838
	45,543 89	71,493 93	101,456 15	187,718 07	260,646 93	359,528 63
	156,299 85	200,722 55	267,462 79	369,567 51	530,097 36	727,129 99
Home	903	778	2,182	2,289	2,069	798
	88,200 00	137,236 00	259,609 00	393,708 00	493,021 00	746,434 00
	199,478 00	277,305 00	418,329 00	627,910 00	890,029 00	453,951 00
Germania	284	722	2,382	3,071	4,623	5,007
	39,571 98	58,326 43	137,134 72	250,374 08	442,521 70	743,746 29
	202,471 69	260,885 43	335,342 13	500,411 49	800,230 39	1,240,299 65
Security	....	211	1,888	1,403	2,134	3,328
	....	23,423 00	80,538 00	149,411 00	323,827 00	603,651 00
	....	122,857 00	160,092 00	249,831 00	425,027 00	757,398 00
North America	....		1,040	1,236	2,368	3,790
	....	Organized.	125,474 07	229,671 18	649,579 84	1,303,566 61
	....		160,853 12	285,142 05	706,742 63	1,539,019 26

John Hancock		Organized.	140	531	596	715
						$286,067 00
			$115,257 54	$207,515 42	$318,650 42	$524,506 00
Globe Mutual				1,039	2,763	3,051
				133,965 13	417,737 29	672,429 07
				218,384 27	469,009 12	789,248 62
Widows and Orphans'				105	1,093	1,582
				17,259 19	107,138 70	248,957 00
				231,538 76	306,814 01	530,839 00
Continental (Conn.)				72	525	1,524
				6,039 99	61,499 74	195,619 50
						490,013 59
National (N. Y.)				17	482	706
					96,710 78	158,801 63
					182,309 32	206,707 47
Brooklyn				272	817	1,207
				38,156 97	92,397 13	260,012 64
				160,738 10	218,091 18	404,411 52
Universal					656	1,555
					71,694 90	227,836 45
					243,360 41	315,904 22
Connecticut General					14	662
					* 5,681 43	65,524 83
					† 112,447 56	543,424 86
Continental (N. Y.)						†† 1,705
						238,092 00
						73,299 00

* From October 1, 1865, to December 31, 1866. † Commenced business October 1, 1865. †† 8 months.

ORIGIN AND BUSINESS OF COMPANIES—CONTINUED.

	1861.	1862.	1863.	1864.	1865.	1866.
Great Western						
						$89,823 00
						$55,539 00
American Popular						
						50,829 00
						149,676 00
Atlantic Mutual						905
						78,634 00
						175,779 57
New York State						752
						48,150 72
						155,765 15
New Jersey Mutual						* 857
					Organized.	* 8,577 92
						166,142 95
Provident (Phila.)						† 528
						82,531 70
						205,528 31

* Total since organization. † Incorporated third month 22d, 1865. Commenced business seventh month, 1865.

NOTES

To the foregoing Records of the Business of Companies.

NOTE 1.—Where the word "organized," in the totals above, does not appear, the organization took place during the year under which the figures first occur.

NOTE 2.—From the impossibility of getting statistics, no companies are embraced in the foregoing which are not doing business in New York or Massachusetts. This is the only full tabular statement that has ever been compiled; and, like all the book, it is copyrighted. These tables are a study, and, in many respects, are valuable and suggestive. As will be seen, they have cost not a little of labor and careful painstaking.

www.ingramcontent.com/pod-product-compliance
Lightning Source LLC
LaVergne TN
LVHW021402110826
845150LV00007B/1744

* 9 7 8 1 4 2 5 5 1 2 7 2 9 *